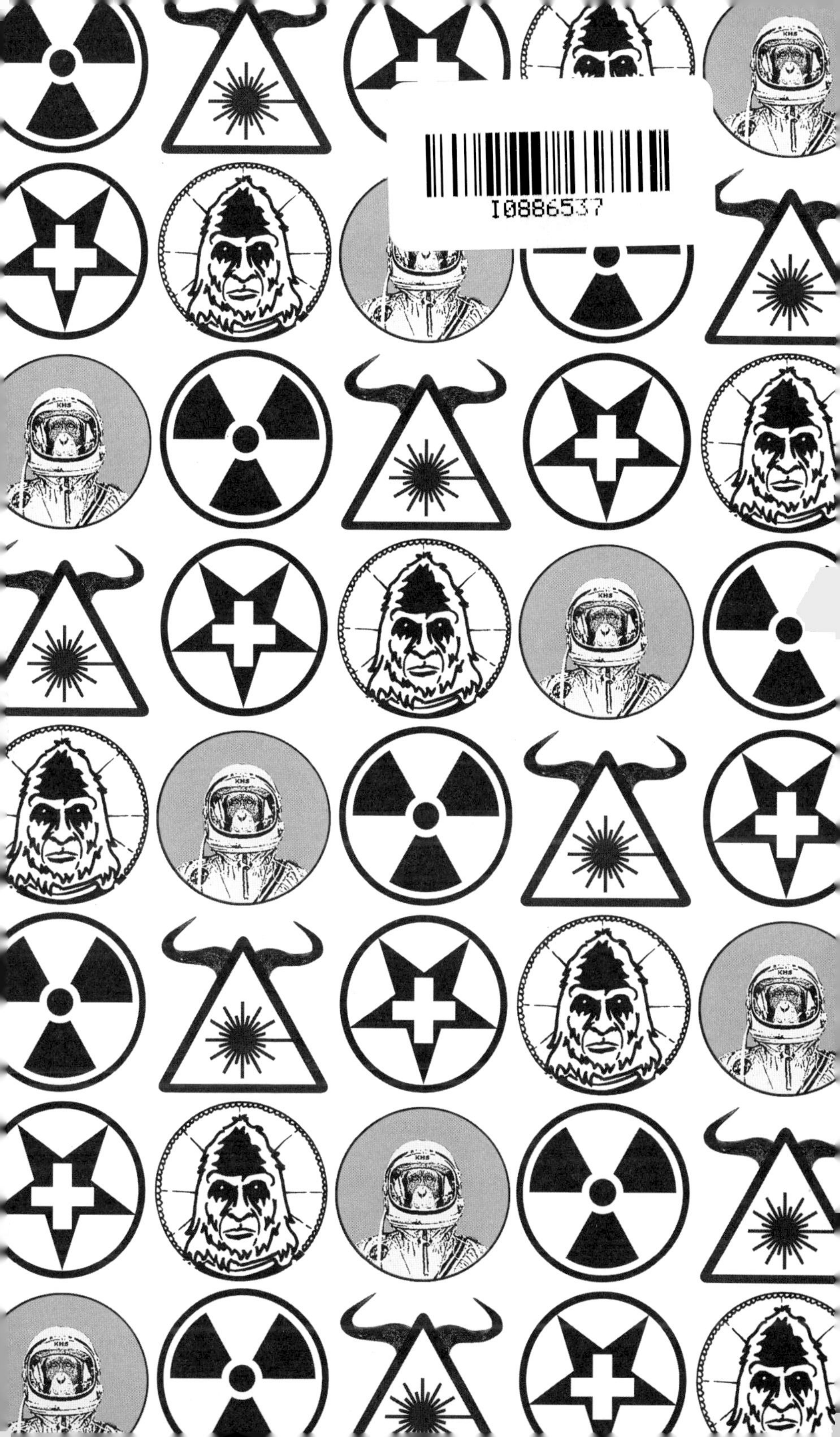

SHARED UNIVERSE

ALSO BY PAUL VERMEERSCH

POETRY

Shared Universe: New and Selected Poems 1995–2020 (2020)
Self-Defence for the Brave and Happy (2018)
Don't Let It End Like This Tell Them I Said Something (2014)
The Reinvention of the Human Hand (2010)
Between the Walls (2005)
The Fat Kid (2002)
Burn (2000)

CHAPBOOKS

Further Communiqués from the Imaginary World (2019)
Imaginary Poems (ca. 2016)
The Technology of the Future Will Emerge Hungry (2013)
Widows & Orphans (2002)
What You Wish Wasn't True (1999)

ANTHOLOGIES

The Al Purdy A-Frame Anthology (2009)
The I.V. Lounge Reader (2001)

SHARED UNIVERSE

NEW AND SELECTED POEMS 1995–2020

PAUL VERMEERSCH

INTRODUCTION BY DANIEL SCOTT TYSDAL

ECW

Published by ECW Press
665 Gerrard Street East
Toronto, Ontario, Canada M4M 1Y2
416-694-3348 / info@ecwpress.com

MISFIT

Editor for the Press: Michael Holmes / a misFit book
Cover design: Michel Vrana
Cover image: © KRK Ryden
Author photo: © Meg Matera Photography

LIBRARY AND ARCHIVES CANADA CATALOGUING IN PUBLICATION

Title: Shared universe : new and selected poems, 1995–2020 / Paul Vermeersch ; introduction by Daniel Scott Tysdal.

Other titles: Poems. Selections

Names: Vermeersch, Paul, author. | Tysdal, Daniel Scott, 1978– writer of introduction.

Identifiers: Canadiana (print) 20200232401
Canadiana (ebook) 20200232487

ISBN 978-1-77041-224-8 (hardcover)
ISBN 978-1-77090-400-2 (PDF)
ISBN 9781770903999 (ePUB)

Classification: LCC PS8593.E74 A6 2020
DDC C811/.54—dc23

The publication of *Shared Universe* has been generously supported by the Canada Council for the Arts which last year invested $153 million to bring the arts to Canadians throughout the country and is funded in part by the Government of Canada. *Nous remercions le Conseil des arts du Canada de son soutien. L'an dernier, le Conseil a investi 153 millions de dollars pour mettre de l'art dans la vie des Canadiennes et des Canadiens de tout le pays. Ce livre est financé en partie par le gouvernement du Canada.* We acknowledge the support of the Ontario Arts Council (OAC), an agency of the Government of Ontario, which last year funded 1,737 individual artists and 1,095 organizations in 223 communities across Ontario for a total of $52.1 million. We also acknowledge the contribution of the Government of Ontario through the Ontario Book Publishing Tax Credit, and through Ontario Creates for the marketing of this book.

ONTARIO CREATES

ONTARIO ARTS COUNCIL
CONSEIL DES ARTS DE L'ONTARIO
an Ontario government agency
un organisme du gouvernement de l'Ontario

Canada Council for the Arts
Conseil des Arts du Canada
Canada

PRINTED AND BOUND IN CANADA

PRINTING: FRIESENS 5 4 3 2 1

MIX
Paper from responsible sources
FSC www.fsc.org FSC® C016245

1 2 3 4 5 6 7 8 9 0

A B C D E F G H I J

K L M N O P Q R S T

U V W X Y Z @ # & *

CONTENTS

INTRODUCTION

PSALMS OF THE METAOCCULT

APPARATUS AND PROCEDURES FOR THE IMAGINARY WORLD

SUBURBAN HAUNTOLOGY

CREATURES OF ANOTHER ARK

(POST)HUMAN ORIGIN STORIES

REQUIRED MODIFICATIONS FOR THE TRANSHUMAN

MORE POEMS OF PROPHECY AND CLAIRVOYANCE

THE IMAGINARY WORLD IS NOW AVAILABLE IN YOUR CHOICE OF TWO OR THREE DIMENSIONS

QUICKLY, INTO THE LIGHTVERSE!

INTRODUCTION

SHIPS, SILENCES, AND SANCTUARIES: ON PAUL VERMEERSCH'S *SHARED UNIVERSE*

BY DANIEL SCOTT TYSDAL

1. INTO THE VERMEERSCHVERSE

It was Paul who introduced me to the other Pauls.

In early April of 2019, we met at Tibet Kitchen in the Parkdale neighbourhood of Toronto to discuss *Shared Universe*, his book of new and selected poems. He asked if I would be interested in writing the introduction, and of course I jumped at the opportunity.

I have long been an admirer of Paul's poetry, and I was keen to introduce readers to the traits and features I value and esteem.

First and foremost, of course, is Vermeersch's expert work with the tools of his trade: images that immerse and stir, metaphors and similes that illuminate and surprise, language that in its music can enrapt and lift or in its cadence can inflect personality and generate mood, and voices and forms that in their variety make the collection choral. These are just a few of the skills that lead Karl Jirgens to celebrate Vermeersch's "luminous turns of language" and Jason Wiens to praise his "remarkable virtuosity and range."

Just as important as Vermeersch's work with these tools is what he accomplishes with this artistic labour. I think of this achievement as two interrelated modes of illumination.

The first mode is best summed up by Amy Lavender Harris, who writes that "by exposing the tensions that stretch not only between individuals but between cultures, species, and even epochs—Vermeersch shows us one way to navigate that difficult pathway between being and meaning." Harris draws our attention to Vermeersch's ability to illuminate our needs and struggles and dreams by probing vast swaths of community, cultural production, and knowledge and his capacity to shed new light on these communities (from the suburban to the planetary to the spiritual), cultural creations (from the pop to the high), and fields of knowledge (from history to science to the MetaOccult, i.e., Vermeersch's term for those fake religions, mock philosophies, and made-up observances we recognize as fictions and fabrications that nonetheless offer a kind of spiritual gratification).

The second mode of illumination, most clearly present in Vermeersch's recent work, is best characterized by Mark Mothersbaugh's claim that Vermeersch's poems provide "nothing less than a manual for navigating the current landscape of booby traps and hidden unravelling" and R.M. Vaughan's lauding Vermeersch's poetry as "part inspirational tract (borne of a deliciously playful inspiration, not the usual kind), part prophetic revelation." Here, we find commended Vermeersch's willingness to cast a light that reveals the darkness of our bleak, regressive times and his eagerness to not give in, to cast another light that shines a path through this darkness.

At Tibet Kitchen, I started to share these thoughts with Paul, eager to discuss how they might take shape in an introduction, when Paul revealed he had a surprise for me. He withdrew a Manila envelope, handed it to me across the table, and dropped my jaw.

I did not recognize any of the books listed in the *Shared Universe* table of contents. In place of the collections that I had read, from *Burn* to *Self-Defence for the Brave and Happy*, I found unfamiliar titles like *Psalms of the MetaOccult* and *Creatures of Another Ark*. Marvelling, I rifled through the envelope's contents: photocopies of book covers bearing Paul's name along with unfamiliar titles—*Suburban Hauntology* and *(Post)Human Origin Stories*; shots of people bearing Paul's image, a woman in a T-shirt with a cartoon drawing of Paul, his eyes redacted by a black rectangle; a man's forearm tattooed with Paul's visage, his mouth replaced by a blank line; and photos of Paul that were not quite Paul—Paul in a director's chair, Paul wearing a baseball cap, Paul dressed in rags, a wasteland stretching into the distance behind him.

"These are top secret," Paul said. "Be careful with them."

As I leafed through the documents, he explained that with *Shared*

Universe he wished to break free of the limiting conventions of the New and Selected. He did not want to simply provide the most exemplary poems, ordered chronologically by collection. Instead, he needed to reveal the unwritten books hidden within his books.

"In this universe," he said, "time is thematic instead of chronological. Space is aesthetic instead of voluminous."

"So, in this New and Selected," I said, pausing as I tried to put the pieces together, "you're giving life to the Pauls who could have been."

Paul shook his head, gesturing to the documents in front of me.

"Right. You've gone further than simply reordering your poems."

"I have." He grinned.

"These are the collections of other Pauls, other versions of you."

Paul, the one across the table from me, nodded.

"Does this mean that in order to write this introduction, I not only have to journey through your poems, but I have to travel to other universes?"

Paul asked the waiter for the bill.

2. *SHARED UNIVERSE* AND RENEWING THE NEW AND SELECTED

I left that meeting uncertain and confused. Why wasn't Paul publishing a traditional, chronological New and Selected? And how had he been able to venture to these other universes? When I returned home and read Vermeersch's thematically, aesthetically organized New and Selected, I found the answer to these questions.

Before getting to these answers, I first want to compare Vermeersch's unconventional organizational method to the traditional New and Selected. The convention of the genre is that poets order their poems chronologically by collection. With Vermeersch's unusual approach, we do lose one feature of the customary method: the ability to track his development as a poet. We are not given the chance to chart the evolution of his work from narrative autobiographical realism (*Burn*, *The Fat Kid*, *Between the Walls*) to a more imagistic, inventive, and visionary mode concerned with the arc of civilization from its origin (*The Reinvention of the Human Hand*) to its collapse (*Don't Let It End Like This Tell Them I Said Something*) to its reimagining (*Self-Defence for the Brave and Happy*). At the same time, though, we do not lose the more important feature of the traditional New and Selected: the opportunity to read exemplary poems by a talented, distinctive, and prescient poet.

This small loss, the capacity to chart Vermeersch's evolution as a poet, is minor compared to what is gained through his unique approach to the New and Selected. Why, then, has Vermeersch ordered his New and Selected by idea and mode of expression, gathering the poems under new titles in alternate collections? What, exactly, is gained?

First, with this new order, Vermeersch is able to foreground four types of poems interspersed throughout his oeuvre: prophetic poems, poems of the imagination, poems of hybridity, and poems of transition and transformation. There is, of course, complex variety within Vermeersch's examples of these types of poems and intricate interplay between the categories. However, this ordering method does, nonetheless, allow Vermeersch to emphasize specific practices of reflection, vision, creation, and connection that are crucial to his project. In other words, sacrificing the evolutionary tale of the traditional linear New and Selected, Vermeersch engenders a clearer vision and profounder experience of his project as a poet.

Second, this reordering does not happen in a vacuum. Yes, Vermeersch foregrounds four types of poems, but he very consciously foregrounds these specific types of poems in opposition to the ignorance, injustice, and violence that characterizes the rising Dark Age of our times, what Vermeersch calls the "Great Regression." Poems are not just words and sounds and meanings. Poems are lenses. Poems are shields. Poems are ships and silences and sanctuaries. And these precisely selected poems, the processes of perception, imagination, and creation their reordering centres, offer the lenses and shields and sails we need today to endure, resist, and change.

Third, on this note of change, the willingness to diverge from tradition that underpins Vermeersch's renewal of the New and Selected is itself a gain. "This 'new and selected poems,'" as A.F. Moritz astutely puts it, "is in fact a metamorphosis itself, an altogether new work, because here the book as a whole is the unit of composition." By taking the book as a unit of composition, Vermeersch reminds us that the ethos of courage and flexibility, of sustaining transformation arising out of careful attention, honest reflection, and radical imaginative leaps, practised and promoted by the poems cannot simply end where the poems end. This ethos must also operate beyond the poems at the level of the collection itself, and, by extension, beyond the collection in the lives we live and the world we share.

Finally, these three gains combine to create the final achievement of Vermeersch's ordering of *Shared Universe*: the capacity, through the poems, to travel to other universes. How? This arises out of our ability to imagine these other universes, our readiness to experience them as real, our openness to travel. How do I know this? Because, in order to more intimately introduce you to the art and value of Vermeersch's prophetic poems, poems of the imagination, poems of hybridity, and poems of transition and transformation, I travelled to a number of these other universes and met these alternate Pauls. These poems are portals, gateways, and I stepped through.

Before sharing my inter-universe travels with you, I want to make one final summative reflection on Vermeersch's renewal of the New and Selected. The loss is academic. By not ordering this book chronologically by collection, Vermeersch stops us from painting a series of portraits of the artist as a linearly developing entity. By contrast, through this new order, through this gathering of poems by idea and mode of expression, the gains are not only academic or artistic. This approach does not simply reflect Paul's personality or provide a handy marketing tool. Instead, the gains for us, as readers, are aesthetic and practical, are readerly and revolutionary. We experience the joy, hurt, wonder, and awareness that arise when we immerse ourselves in the work of a gifted, distinctive artist, and, just as importantly, we become intimate with the vision and tools necessary to witnessing, encountering, opposing, and transforming our dark times.

In the ensuing sections of my introduction, then, I will show how this is true by illuminating Vermeersch's poetry through the different universes *Shared Universe* carried me to, the various Pauls his poems connected me with. I will prove this is the case by giving myself over to the combination of imagination, belief, and creation Vermeersch's poetry promotes. By delving into what makes Vermeersch's poetry tick, the ingenuity of its art and the force of its insight, emotion, and sensation, I will reveal how his particular ticking sustains and spurs us as beings who share this universe, makers united in this work to foretell and devise, to connect and transform, to revive lost homes and build new ones.

3. "WHATEVER CREATURE IS REQUIRED": VERMEERSCH'S PROPHAGOGY

To help me understand Vermeersch's prophetic poems, I travelled to one of the universes where these works are gathered in the collections *Psalms of the MetaOccult* and *More Poems of Prophecy and Clairvoyance*. This bleak, oppressive, totalitarian world, I discovered, had outlawed Vermeersch's poetry. Nano-boards and bio-ads everywhere flashed the following icons:

Thankfully, in the cracks of this brutal regime, I also found evidence that a resistance flourished: smashed nano-boards, bio-ads infected and illegible, border walls splashed with graffiti quoting Paul's poems along with the prophetic works of other poets. Following these signs, I managed to connect with a small but dedicated band of rebels, or, more accurately, I managed to get myself kidnapped by these rebels. Even though I proved myself to be a friend when I showed them my printout of *Shared Universe*, they still refused to remove their masks, let alone take me to meet their universe's Paul.

What they did share with me were their bootleg copies of Vermeersch's books and their hand-scrawled pamphlets dedicated to his work. I was not surprised to see that many of these pamphlets contained interpretations of, and reflections on, Vermeersch's predictions. However, I was especially struck by the fact that a significant number of these texts, drawing on Vermeersch's poetry, also provided advice on how to undertake one's own work of prophecy, how to commit to the labour of learning, connecting, resisting, and inspiring that prophecy requires.

The rebel in the plague mask illuminated for me why this was the case. Yes, she explained, Vermeersch's prophetic poems contain acts of divining and foretelling, flares of forewarning and prediction. Yet what distinguishes them as a group is the significant work Vermeersch does in exploring the full range of prophetic voices and strategies while also interrogating the very practice of prophecy. The result is a sort of prophet bootcamp.

The rebel in the Sasquatch mask added that they valued Vermeersch because he does not aim to rise above the world as the lone all-seeing knower. Instead, he demonstrates the value of this form of envisioning and expression, and, at the same time, he encourages us to undertake this same work, which demands our sincere attention and requires us to imagine and mull, to challenge and care. Vermeersch, then, employs the full range of his poetic tools to provide fertile models of composition and to spur us to take part in the prophetic act.

When I returned safely to our universe and turned to our Paul's prophetic poems, I found the rebels' insights to be accurate and illuminating. Take, for example, Vermeersch's work with one of the most foundational tools of poetry — imagery, particularly the repeated specific images in "I Am Happy to Live in an Age of Plenty": "painkillers," "ammunition," "meat," and "children." In their repetition and interconnection, these images compose a sort of arithmetic equation that we as readers complete. Each of these elements in surplus, particularly "one child [. . .] for every round of ammunition," equals society-collapsing violence.

With similar ingenuity, Vermeersch uses simile and metaphor to not only name the unnameable but to make us active in comprehending, imagining, and sensing these figures. In the "2: Machine" canto of the erasure poem "The Technology of the Future Will Emerge Hungry," the charging steed is "like a balloon, like a fire / in the distance" and it "rollicked / across the lake like a bee." This triangulation of similes borders on the sublime as it challenges us to at once grasp the meaning and give ourselves over to not fully knowing. Vermeersch achieves a similar effect with a metaphor and simile combination in canto 2 of "Water": "his eyes are stigmas, / sadly immense like the mirage of a willow." This effect occurs both through the originality of the vision and through the revelation that, staring into the poem's frozen water surface, these eyes could be our very own.

Vermeersch uses another foundational technique of the prophetic tradition: the development of a symbol for the (societal, political, spiritual, etc.) threat, whether looming on the horizon, immediately present, or fallen but threatening to return. In constructing "the old ones" and "Leviathan" in, respectively, "Magog" and "Leviathan," Vermeersch strikes the necessary balance between vital specificity—the particularity required to make the threat's sensory and emotional presence real—and strategic openness, blurring the figure just enough so that its danger can still resonate across communities, regions, and eras. Significantly, through his development of these figures, Vermeersch also focuses on spurring the reader to act. These spurs take the form of two different warnings delivered through two different tactics.

"Magog" is defined by how epically and painfully Vermeersch builds our passivity and compliance in relation to the old ones. In canto 5, "They thrive in our narcolepsy. / They wolf our thoughts. And we want their love," while their tune, in canto 11, "is a music / to betray your neighbours by." Even the rare overt calls to arms, such as the repeated "Look away!" in canto 7, are, really, gestures of inaction, and the poem ends with canto 15 as we lie down with old ones in "[a] darkness that feeds on the absence, / that outlives the message."

In giving such suffocating form to our grim submission, Vermeersch delivers his warning: we must wake and resist.

By contrast, in "Leviathan," Vermeersch warns against losing sight of the figure for the sublime threat, against thinking it can be ignored, sidestepped, or erased. We must constantly push the boundaries of our imaginings and expressions in order to encounter vast and incomprehensible dangers. His technique here is to compose a bounty of metaphors and incarnations for Leviathan, ranging from the opening catalogue of metaphors and the strategy-establishing imperative—"She is a sea serpent, a school crush, / a pop star—whatever creature is required"—to the concluding (supposed) death of Leviathan in canto 3, which results in rebirth: "the many thousands / of her daughters hatching from the salt."

Vermeersch also immerses us in the communities that develop around and through prophecy. "What the Prophecy Could Not Foretell" connects past prophet to present interpreter, revealing how assessing a prophecy's failure provokes both new revelations and uncovers the subtle resonances between the present and the foretold. "The Prophets Want to Know If They Were Close" composes a similar though even more direct connection as the first-person plural prophets speak directly to the reader as prophetic interpreter, asking us if the sky darkened as predicted or if the plague arrived on schedule. Most striking is the poem's provocative final turn in which the directionality of this cross-temporal connection is shifted—"We presume one day you will discover / the means to answer us"—and then broken—"but our vocabulary is already too primitive to understand." With the cento, "Rubble," Vermeersch revels in the choral potential of prophecy by composing with lines borrowed from a hundred-plus sources, ranging from contemporary poems to ancient manuscripts to movie taglines. This gathering of debris takes full, riveting form through his masterful blending of the different sources and the distinct voice and vision that results.

Vermeersch's prophetic poetry, then, is characterized by the range of his poetic strategies and the variety of ways he invites us to reflect on, engage in, and act upon prophecy. It is also distinguished by the way he turns to apocalypse and dystopia not to revel in misery and preach submission, but to express his hopefulness for a better future, the way he, as Brent Raycroft puts it, "explodes stereotypes of both science fiction and future history, especially the false dichotomy of utopia and dystopia."

Not surprisingly, given the scope and ethos of Vermeersch's prophetic poems, in the alternate universe in which his work serves as a foundational prophet pedagogy, or prophagogy, one of the resistance's rallying cries is "Whatever creature is required." This command reminds them that in their work to predict and change, to attend and endure, they must remain nimble and open in vision and creation, in expressing and in listening, in claiming and sharing speech. All prophets are guides, yes, but the best of them guide others to prophesize.

4. "ASSEMBLE!": THE AVENGING IMAGINATION

Travelling universe to universe, I discovered that Vermeersch's poems of the imagination, gathered in the sections *Apparatus and Procedures for the Imaginary World* and *The Imaginary World Is Now Available in Your Choice of Two or Three Dimensions*, are collected together in a number of different realms. In the most unique instance, though, these individual poems are not gathered in book form and Vermeersch is not a poet in our sense of the word. Instead, in this particular universe, Vermeersch is a Hollywood filmmaker in a society where poetry is the most popular form of art and his poems manifest as superhero movie action and dialogue.

I had the opportunity to speak with poet-director Vermeersch, and we were both amazed to discover that his superhero team, The Avengers, exists in our universe as well. However, the more we talked, the more we realized there are extreme differences between the two. Whereas our Avengers use physical superpowers to engage in violent, epic battles, The Avengers in this alternate poetic universe represent different types and activities of the imagination. Their imagination is their power.

Returning to our universe, I found that these alternative universe Avengers provide a fertile means to illuminate the work of the imagination in our Vermeersch's poetry. To accomplish this, I will call on three of poet-director Paul's heroes: the Iron Magination, the Ingenuitious Hulk, and the Scarlet Wit.

Poems of the Iron Magination are poems in which the imagination faces a destabilizing external force—a loss, an injustice, or ignorance, to name a few of the many possibilities. Language and the poet's tools are like Iron Man's suit—a defence and a means of fighting back—and the tension of the poem arises from the encounter between the poet's creations and the poem-animating force that threatens everything from violence to incoherence to silence. Vermeersch's most overt example of this is "Essential Apparatus for the Imaginary World," in which he imagines machinic and sartorial means to counter everything from economic inequality to societal regression.

Looking under the hood of the first section of this poem, "1: Patent for Economic Equality Engine," reveals the sophistication and nuance of Vermeersch's approach. This section provides an apparently objective, detached description of the economic equality engine: a guillotine-laden "thirteen-sided polyhedron / cast in mirror-finish platinum." Through this description, Vermeersch is able to succinctly and powerfully give form to the brutality and scale of economic inequality, suggesting both the level of ingenuity needed to confront this vast inequity and the potential magnitude of the violence of revolutionary action.

Crucially, through his imaginative work, he suffuses this seemingly objective description with a sense of unease that, with a moment of reflection, delivers the shock of horror. He accomplishes this by crafting and arranging images that oscillate between buoyant lift and terrifying plummet. This occurs with Vermeersch's description of the twelve blades, which, to give a few examples, are shaped like "a subpoena, a kite feather, [and] a marlin fin." The bounty and range of these similes creates a lyric escape, the mind swirling in the sensory plenitude and symbolic potential of the different shapes. However, this flight is countered by the reminder that these shapes are blades committed to extreme acts of violence. Vermeersch creates a similar effect when he observes that the machine "can be programmed to snap its blades / shut in sequence, producing / melodies" and play "'Gassenhauer,' for example." He creates the lift-plummet oscillation here by linking Carl Orff's hopeful, playful composition to the snapping guillotine blade as a musical instrument.

Poems of the Ingenuitious Hulk are similar to poems of the Iron Magination in that these poems face a destabilizing force. However, the force here is internal not external, and language and the poet's tools are dedicated to capturing the intricacies of this struggle, the way the same body contains both Bruce Banner struggling against the Hulk and the Hulk struggling against Banner. "Basic Instructions for Anaesthesia" deals with personal trauma, which, in canto 2, is described as a thought, "[l]ike spoilt flesh" that "becomes infected, incurable." This trauma is the "something best / forgotten: birthdays turned necrotic, / a marriage, a festering assault." Vermeersch captures this struggle between forgetting a trauma and experiencing its pain by figuring the trauma as physical hurt: a rotted tooth in canto 1 and an injured leg in need of amputation in canto 2. Though he gestures to pre-surgery anaesthetics for both, "laughing gas" and "[w]hiskey," respectively, he embellishes both the injury's pain and the grisliness of the treatment, an imagistic abundance that shows just how impossible it is to follow the anesthetizing advice of the poem's refrain: "The idea is not to feel. The idea is to forget." Here, Vermeersch repeats the warning he delivers in "Magog," but in relation to trauma, foregrounding the danger of submission and the importance of the work to resist.

Whereas poems of the Iron Magination and Ingenuitious Hulk are characterized by their relationship to the poem-animating force, poems of the Scarlet Wit are distinguished less by the subject the imagination encounters and more by the processes of the imagination. The Scarlet Witch's power of reality manipulation manifests at the level of the imagination through the Scarlet Wit's ability to extrapolate and recombine. This is the imagination that seems to generate something out of nothing, to reveal that everything contains so much more than lazy glances and everyday reflection suggests.

In "Mixing Grey: A Practical Guide for Painters," Vermeersch studies a seemingly bland and lifeless subject: grey, which, as a colour, lacks boldness and vibrancy and, as an adjective, means boring or sad. However, through his extrapolating and expanding imaginative work, he reveals the sensory, emotional, and symbolic vigour contained in these different greys. He achieves this through a two-part structure that he repeats grey after grey: first, an original and surprising image-rich description of the specific grey, and, second, an equally unexpected explanation of which items to mix in order to create this colour, recipes that stir through both their novelty and their impossibility.

The recombinative powers of the Scarlet Wit are best demonstrated in "The Modernist Canon," the whole-poem anagrams Vermeersch created from canonical poems by William Carlos Williams, Ezra Pound, and Wallace Stevens. Through this process, he crafts two new texts: his wonderfully bizarre original poems, which stand on their own, and the insights generated by reading the new poem and the canonical source side by side.

Like the Avengers of our universe, these Avengers of the imagination employ the same gathering battle cry: "Assemble!" However, whereas our Avengers undertake this work of assembling to combat villains in a black-and-white, win-or-lose battle, these other Avengers encounter a wide range of destabilizing forces and creative potentials in interactions that seek to linguistically preserve, connect, and reveal. Whereas our Avengers repeat, again and again, the same *smash*, *bang*, *boom*, these other, poetic Avengers aim to originate and renew in their assembling. And whereas our Avengers seat us to passively witness their big screen exploits, these other Avengers invite us to assemble with them, to take part in the act of understanding, envisioning, and creating.

At the level of the lifework, one of the ways Vermeersch counts himself as a member of these imaginative Avengers, and one of the ways these poems of the imagination connect to his prophetic poems, is in his promotion of the MetaOccult. Spiritual fulfillment,

Vermeersch argues, can be achieved through active make-believe and appreciating products of the imagination, even when we understand and accept that these things are not real. The imagination itself, for him, is real enough.

At the level of the poem, one of the many ways Vermeersch joins these Avengers, and, in turn, encourages us to encounter the MetaOccult, is by foregrounding this interactive quality in his imaginative works through his favouring of forms that advise and encourage our participation: the "Practical Guide," "Basic Instructions," the "How to," and the "Manual for Survivors." These methods move us to take part in this crucial practice: imagining as a means of better understanding and changing what is real.

5. "AN ATLAS OF BAFFLING CHANNELS": BOUNDING BOUNDS

In our universe, the poems of hybridity gathered in *Suburban Hauntology* and *Creatures of Another Ark* manifest most simply as poems that probe the relationships between humans and their habitats (identity, community, landscape, temporal location, etc.) and poems that explore human-animal interactions (physically, linguistically, metaphorically, etc.), respectively. There are a number of alternate universes in which this is also the case, but one in particular stands out. These works exist in that universe not as poems, but as the plans for habitat-transforming and creature-creating projects.

Thankfully, given the strangeness and complexity of this realm, the Paul in this universe was very familiar with our own world. He succinctly explained that the nature of his world's physiological, epistemological, ontological, and technological difference from our own is best summed up by their definition of the word boundary. For him and his people, it means, at the same time, both a barrier and the practice of leaping across borders. This Vermeersch explained that he, thus, labours as their version of a poet, a sort of bioengineer crossed with an architect, farmer, and computer programmer that they call a bounder, and he composes their version of poetry: actual hybrid, amalgam, and chimera environs and entities, many of which we would consider utopic breakthroughs and many of which we would call abominations. Theirs is a world of ancient myth converging with the ultimate advances in technology and consciousness.

Though our universe's Vermeersch is limited by the physical laws, social norms, and technological restrictions of our time, the seeds of this boundary-transcending potential are evident in the poetry of our Paul, making him a sort of proto-version of this other universe's Vermeersch. The poems in *Suburban Hauntology* and *Creatures of Another Ark* take part in this "bounding bounds," both leaping boundaries and observing the bounds placed on leaping. They are packed with examples of this work to reconceive boundaries, disclosing fertile and unexpected interplays or exposing the perimeters where difference and distance remain insurmountable.

Through this work, Vermeersch might not manufacture new beings and habitats in the physical world. However, he does reveal the new, strange, and unconventional creatures we become or construct when we travel the passages and channels that at once link us to and separate us from our pasts, our communities, our environs, and other animals. He catalogues the architecture of the odd homes we fabricate in time and on land. He gathers the strange menagerie of our multiplicitous animal forms.

Take, for example, "Suburban Hauntology: Kitchen Wallpaper." This poem deals with the seemingly simple act of remembering the kitchen wallpaper of a childhood home with its "large yellow flowers / and small brown ones." Vermeersch reveals the full complexity and difficulty of this undertaking by teasing out how the act of remembering conjures the ghosts of the forces that mediate the relationship between the present remembering self and the past remembered object. These perception-shaping ghosts rise up one by one as the poem develops: first, the in-that-moment forces that influenced the perception of the wallpaper, second, the inflection of the perception of the wallpaper through the speaker-as-child's "tiny, unmet desires," third, the growing, suffocating presence of the wallpaper as it takes on physical, gaseous, and sonic volume, and, finally, the perception modulated through a faulty analog TV, the "vertical hold [. . .] malfunctioning."

Vermeersch, then, fashions the figure of the rememberer as one who is haunted, yes, but, more particularly, one who is haunted by layers of perception, ghosts of sensation-shaping lenses. Much of the power of this poem derives from just how dense these spirits make perception, how the wallpaper is distorted and amplified, made surreal and symbolic. This summoning of ghosts alone, which constitutes the first twenty-five of the poem's twenty-seven lines, would make for a potent and rewarding work: this entity his bounding forms captivates and illuminates. However, Vermeersch conjures another, provocative ghost that dwells beyond these ghosts in his closing lines: "You must understand that this is what it was like— / it was *like* this—but this is not how it was." In other words, these many phantoms capture what the experience of this moment was *like*, but they cannot grasp how it really was. This remains fully absent, a sort of ghost-haunting ghost, a massive apparition that prowls the horizon of memory and perception.

Vermeersch also delves into and reworks the boundaries that characterize community identities. The suburban fathers of "Lawn Kings" are lawn kings, of course, because of their dedication to maintaining perfect yards. Vermeersch also figures them as kings who are lawns insofar as community identity is a sort of lawn care: conventional and prescribed, shaping and homogenizing. It provides healthy vehicles for their hate of one another, which manifests in the "triumph" of "thick green carpets" and in the "defeat" of "dry brown patches." It offers the manicuring "argument for decency" that saves them from the wilds of "sin."

In "Boolarandah," Vermeersch fashions out of this convergence of father, son, and toy a sort of familial Cerebus perched on the cusp of the underworld of the "deep hole in the lawn." In this figure, he crystallizes the father-son dynamics of education and power that, to re-appropriate his words, stretch "through centuries deeper than oceans." One of the most striking features of this clan amalgam is the way it crystalizes a moment of fluid identity. The father becomes the child through his playful act, inventing the hole-inhabiting monster and holding his son above it "like bait." The child becomes the father by taking on the role of father in relation to his "toy soldier," which he controls in relation to the hole and throws. Though the toy soldier "floats beyond the fence / to safety in the uncut grass," Vermeersch instills this moment with a fertile ambiguity. Did the child intentionally throw the toy soldier to safety or did he throw it into the hole as a replacement sacrifice, the opening parachute unexpectedly bearing the soldier free of the monster? And how does his choice reflect on his understanding of, and hope for, his father's choice?

A similar trading of identity occurs in one of Vermeersch's explorations of the boundaries between self and environment, "Calvin Little and the City of Boys." In the untouched woods at the edge of the suburbs, the boys "build a city in the trees." This liminal space between nature and city is, for them, "civilization." Their civilization is characterized not by human domination but in the ways that the human becomes nature, becomes animal: Calvin is "a monkey," "lighter than leaves," "leaf-light" in his leap, and the nails he grips in his pocket feel like "the evolution of claws." This hybrid Calvin, in turn, inhabits a hybrid environment, sitting "astride the burly biceps of an oak" and endangered by the subdivisions that "will uncurl their asphalt fronds."

"As It Is on the Edge of Town" takes a more geological approach in the meeting of self and environmental boundary. Here, in "the undeveloped fields," "in that margin / where the city almost ends," Vermeersch exposes the vast strata of identities piled one on top of the other in a single location. This area is a dump where "people / aren't afraid to leave their trash," and "a shining white orchard / of cast-off refrigerators." It is also a kind of work of art because this edge of the town is defamiliarized "by the reports of an escaped peacock," and it is an almost-graveyard because of the dead boy discovered there. It is also both a failed development, "the land on which the shopping mall / was never built," and the site of nurtured development, children coming there to fly kites, "to witness movement in the heavens, / to witness colour, / and to feel that they control it."

Vermeersch's animal poems compose a wide range of these chimerical meldings of human and animal; these transformation of one by the other are designed to nurture compassion and understanding. In "Lambs," the symbolic and sentient innocence of the lamb floods into "you," the second-person addressee, after "you" reach through the fence to "lay your hands upon the lamb." The mid-poem feeling of being "wolfish" gives way to a sobbing union as "the faint lines of turquoise, the veins at your temples, [flood] quietly with their blood." "The Animals We Imagine" similarly transform and empower us, even if these creatures evade us in reality. They are vehicles for us to reimagine what we are, what we can in reality become. Animal and human artfully unite in the persona poem "Dogstar," which is dedicated to, and spoken in the voice of, Laika, the first animal in space, while "Notes Toward a Lexicon of the Language of the Bear" poignantly reveals the complexity and richness of "bearish tongue."

In the opening of this section, I observed that Vermeersch reveals the new, strange, and unconventional creatures we become or construct when we travel the passages and channels that at once link us to and separate us from our pasts, our communities, our environs, and other animals. I chose the words "passage" and "channel" inspired by Vermeersch. His "visible man" in the "2: The Glass Door" section of "Suburban Hauntology: On the Interpretation of Front Doors" serves as a kind of embodiment of the world deeply attended to, the world Vermeersch preserves and animates in his poems: "There are no secret / passages. There is only the visible man [. . .] / [. . .] an atlas of baffling channels." This figure is a kind of guiding model for the alt-universe bounders and Vermeersch in his own work with boundaries, a reminder that even in the face of puzzles and silences, of difficulty and strangeness, there are always more passages to read and traverse, more channels for us to travel and flip.

6. "I BECAME A SHAPE-CHANGER": THE POST-POST-

The poems collected in *(Post)Human Origin Stories* and *Required Modifications for the Transhuman* explore our moments of transition and

transformation at the level of people, society, and species, with a focus, as the titles suggest, on the origins of our future in our distant past and on these moments of shifting across, beyond, or through ourselves. Not surprisingly, given this focus on transformation and transition, on the post- and the trans-, these poems manifest in various universes as post-poetry, poetry that has changed into different forms of composition and consumption, of sustenance and dissemination. Just as the speaker in section 2 of "I Became a Wooden Ark the Lives of Animals Filled Me" "became a shape-changer" when toys as identity-giving influences failed to provide a true identity, so does poetry in these other universes become a shape-changer when what is possible allows it or what is needed demands it. Poetry, in other words, is an entity full of change that, itself, is open to change.

Given the centrality of healing/[synonym] to Vermeersch's work, the _____ of _____ [better world], I will share my exploits in the universes in which healing is at the core of poetry's evolution. For example, in one world, Vermeersch is a chemist and his poetry is a kind of pharmacology. I approached this version of Vermeersch with symptoms of disconnection and ennui and he prescribed me "The Painted Beasts of Lascaux." Not the words on the page, but four hoof-shaped yellow ochre pills. I took the pills and my disconnection gave way to connection, my ennui to energy as I felt in my blood "the abiding chant of the hundred billion dead / who came before," their song "trying to pound its way free" from my heart. Along with instilling this eon-spanning connection preserved in Vermeersch's images, the pill also somehow managed to stir the imperative of his single word sentence, "Listen," and capture the buoyancy of his music in lines like "a molecule / a memory of muscled, brawling bulls entombed / deep within."

There are many other examples of this therapeutic-focused transformation of poetry across many universes. In one realm, poetry is a prosthetic. The poem "The Reinvention of the Human Hand," for example, takes the form of a new hand we can wear to take hold of both a hand's absence and its simple activities, needs, and quenchings. Poems are organs in another universe. "Twenty-One Days with a

Baboon Heart," Vermeersch's poem for Baby Fae, the first subject of a xenotransplant procedure, is a heart that can be implanted beside our own to allow us to feel the distinctive beat of "our primordial reflections," the way "[t]hey face and fight and fear what we cannot know." Finally, in another universe, poems are advanced medical devices. Here, Vermeersch constructed "Required Modifications for the Transhuman" as an evolution-accelerating machine. A traveller simply steps into the device, the programmer enters information about the conditions of the environment or planet to which the traveller will venture, and then, within minutes, the traveller's body has made the necessary adaptations.

Returning to our universe of poems composed of words on pages and screens, I am amazed at how closely the effects, influences, and powers of his page poems match those of these other medium-breaking poetries. In Vermeersch's lines, I can feel that heart, that hand, that drumming blood. Through this effect, we see that a turn to the "post-" does not mean turn away from human meaning, dignity, or community. For Vermeersch, the recognition of our post- or trans-human dimensions reveals an expansion of the meaning of human, not a dilution of it. This is one of the aspects of Vermeersch's project that spurred Shelagh Rogers to observe, "Poetry and futurism are both visionary genres, but they don't often go hand in hand. Unless you're Paul Vermeersch." Here, Rogers promotes Vermeersch not as a human-erasing, war-hungry F.T. Marinetti, but as a Buckminster Fuller whose visions are guided by global-mindedness and fellow feeling.

Vermeersch's poems of transition and transformation also show us that every poem is a kind of meta-poem, a poem about, or one that hints at, what poetry could be beyond marked surfaces, words, and sounds. The transformations and transitions, the boundaries and tensions, that play out within a poem, in turn, echo throughout poetry as such, suggesting all it cannot be but could be, pointing to all it never will be but might be. This moves us to ask: if poetry could be another way elsewhere, why is it not like that here? Or wonder: maybe it is that way here. Then why can't we see it?

7. INTO THE ILLUMINATING TURNS

It is appropriate that our universe's Paul ends *Shared Universe*, this impressive testament to his life's work so far, with a selection of light verse. This punctuation point is another sign of Vermeersch's dedication to following his vision and interests, rather than chasing trends and fashions. These works of light verse also highlight many of Vermeersch's strengths as a poet: his imagistic precision and imagination, his finely tuned ear, and the range of his developmental structures and voices.

We see here, too, his capacity to put the light and dark in tension, to spring from the playful to the magnificent or the sublime, through, for example, the doomsday machine in "Little Fatso." We also encounter once again Vermeersch's invitation of his reader to join him as co-creator. Like one of the alt-universe poetic Avengers, he calls us to assemble and assemble with him, to participate in the act of creation. He achieves this through the multiple choice blank for us to fill in "The Fortunate Queen" and through the chilling redaction in the collection-closing "Hush."

These two core features—Vermeersch's dynamic work with a range of tensions and his nurturing of collaboration with the reader—also recommend another reason light verse serves as such an ideal conclusion to this collection. As dark as his subjects often are, the phrase "light verse" sums up so much of Vermeersch's project here in *Shared Universe* and in the creations of all the other possible Pauls. All of this work is "light" insofar as it illuminates and guides, seeks knowledge and shuns ignorance. And this work is "verse" in the word's etymological sense: to turn, to bend—to veer from the expected insight and prescribed path, to cross boundaries and build protections, to forecast the past and renew the future, to delve into the depths of our struggles and pains and to lift into the realm of the imagination.

What stands out for me in Vermeersch's poetry as "light verse," as illuminating turns, is that it is distinguished by a tirelessness, openness, generosity, and wonder that arises from a place of love. In other words, Vermeersch's work with prophagogy, the avenging imagination, bounding bounds, and the post-post- is underpinned by the effort and ardour required to acknowledge, construct, and imagine a truly shared universe. This love is perhaps most explicitly and enthusiastically expressed in "I Feel Love: Hi-NRG," a playful, celebratory, affectionate, and soaring launch off of Donna Summer's seminal collaboration with Giorgio Moroder, "I Feel Love." Two lines in particular could serve as mottos for Vermeersch's poetics: "I feel / love in the collaboration—finish this sentence: / I feel love ______" and "I feel love / for the story that / loops back on itself, that loops back on itself / and is told anew [. . .]."

This love in collaboration and love in looping within and renewing art extends not only through this collection but also throughout Vermeersch's larger body of work as an editor, visual artist, publisher, musical collaborator, teacher, mentor, community builder, and, even, founder of a Holy Order. This love and its artistic extensions are why I leapt at the opportunity to introduce these poems. Sharing myself with this shared universe, accepting its offerings, I have been edified in a way that broadens and sustains, linked to original connections that encourage journeys, tensions that nurture probing, and immersed in an art that prompts new creations. This love is what awaits you in the pages that follow, an invitation to ____________________________ and a call to

DANIEL SCOTT TYSDAL
TORONTO
EARTH-1218
JANUARY 2020

PSALMS OF THE METAOCCULT

SHARED UNIVERSE

I

You and the ice cream truck and the King
Cobra all exist in the same universe
as the two-legged tortoise, the Star Queen Nebula,
and me. Eventually, there must be a story
that involves all six of us: you will be driving
the ice cream truck among the farthest stars
in search of His Majesty King Cobra, despite
his famous venom, despite his propensity
to strike, and I will follow behind you riding
the wounded tortoise, the front wheels
of a plastic Batmobile glued to her shell
as prostheses. These are the forms we will take
when we encounter the Star Queen in her home,
the pillars of creation billowing from her head.

2

And there is King Cobra, coiling his long body
around the pillars, emanating from her third eye
as Uraeus from the forehead of a pharaoh.
"You have come here," he says, "to learn
what you already know: that you exist
in the same universe as ice cream, Batmobiles,
and the act of mutilation." New stars are fusing
within the pillars, and within the stars, new-born
elements: hydrogen, beryllium, carbon, iron . . .
"Use these to make an apple," the serpent says.
"Or make it out of gold, it's all the same." And now
a blind donkey arrives behind us, and a silvery
porpoise, and an immense hypothetical mountain,
and we all nod knowingly, knowing what we know.

PSALMS OF THE METAOCCULT

Psalm 1

Oh hey, Allegèd One, in the armoury
of harmless weapons: there is a pistoleta
that fires tap water [never holy | for Nosferatu],
and a retractable blade in plastic [argent],
in a sheath [sable], a gum spearhead | ready
for self-surrender | and a rifle that launches
seven soft projectiles from a carousel—
Pop! Pop! Pop!—and here, a licorice whip,
and there, a whip of feathers | speaking
of which: behold! The flight simulator and/or
light stimulator. And should the Great
Regression last | there is a battery of pies
for *les entartistes*, but there is no golden apple
marked καλλίστι[1]. Why ever not? Go ask Eris.

1 καλλίστι, kallisti: for the fairest

Psalm 2

I stand upon a Hill. I stand and know everything
the Hill knows. Green'ry and contour of the land,
the ancientness thereabouts, the inscrutable green
filigree of Hill genius, and áll thíngs. Unless,
it's Geoffrey—[S T A T I C]—Then: I am dumb. I know
only the theme song to another century: the clank
of tournament | olden swag | secrets of Game
and Variety, Gong and Show, and as above,
the commercial geists of relative good versus
relative evil. O belovèd Lyceum, what the fuck
is happening? The world will end on X-Day. Say it!
Klaatu barada nikto![2] | Gét sláck! | Ask yourself:
Is eschatology ever that precise? Is epistemology
really all that difficult? Damned if I know. Praise Bob.

---

2 cf. Gort, 1951.

Psalm 3

"And next to of course Bob whatever I
don't know is holy. In the funhouse dark
the bowl of noodles represents the worm
that takes your body everywhere eternal.
You consume | are consumed | the stained
glass window in the *ristorante* says so.
Appetite is the mother of inventory; so list
your desires: *F*, *S*, and *M** | thenceforth
thine idols, say: *Ms.* Amelia Earhart | *Chef* Boy-
árdee | *not* Medusa | *but* her hair. Together
they form a trinity of escape | necessity and
terror: one for the voyage | one for the meal
one for the little god who makes you squeal."

*He spoke. And ate rapidly a bowl of rAmen.

THE TECHNOLOGY OF THE FUTURE WILL EMERGE HUNGRY

1: Phalanx

Often the sun, the pollution, and the lives
of citizens congregating are
no different, invisible until
they come gutted to the concrete.

I watch the furies one morning, my city
nailed, men and women muddy
and crumpled before the
phalanx riding down Yonge Street.

Eight-hundred-odd scared skinny by
the buildings concealing dead bylaws—
the city clogged with swindlers.
We might asphyxiate.

But in the tangle of truth, out of the smog
and empire, we sit down as if our lives were real.

2: Machine

It was like a balloon, like a fire
in the distance. The steed rollicked
across the lake like a bee. There was
never much to fear. Death, yes,
but not the machine that repeated
questions, the cursive alphabet
of a condemned populace.   Why
am I telling you this? It doesn't
really make a difference. The old
mare had the glorious desire
to run, and the river wore a coat
of flamingos. The technology of
the future will emerge hungry
as if all of it had never happened.

3: Balustrade

In spring, a century buckles, pressed
into rusting bed frames, prosthetic legs,
and confused, windswept architecture.
The crows are an accidental beauty.

In autumn, the world was no longer
a phosphorescent empire, fragile
and finite. How simple the future is.
Everything already exists. The tree.

The sky. The elegance of the balustrade
in the hot, thin air. The little island
of beaches ringed in purple fields.

Beneath the structures, the summer
weeds deepen. In dry leaves, the remains
of a fallen figure—she was already ruined.

4: Winter

Suddenly and certainly, the hunter
is aware of the little deaths
overwhelming the secret winter,
the birds of the white blizzard
fallen, the holiday forgotten.

Some were human beings I knew.
They were children in a radiance
of swords, in the last exaltation
of the memorized anthem, a murmur
in a language I must have known.

Suddenly and certainly, in winter,
the world rippled to recognition.
It was the little moment when the snow
fell with the thunder of the news.

5: Tidal Wave

I might have sprung from the seafloor
off California or Alaska. Today,
my brother will be an earthquake.

I speak to anything afloat or on shore,
a herringbone or barefoot girl.
The earthquake reminds us how quiet.

I understand the flotsam you ignore.
A sailboat breaks on an island,
losing its clarity. I look for some fragment

of an anchor so I can tell its origin.
Oceanographers know only reef and water
and all that is vaguely Latin.

I am the true misnomer, six hours nearer
than the hoodoo light guttering behind.

6: Nothing

April snow stopped in the mountains,
failed by winter, stopped in the air,
framed by a savagely still wind.

Nothing nothing nothing nothing
shall rush the wind. The loitering
blast crept softly through winter, blind

and bored and tired. The indifference
crept along, a whining white tar
on the sands. Nothing came out

of the deep windward silence.
If only there were a murmur,
a whisper, voices in the grass,

the wind's aethereal rumours
gaily falling against my ruins.

7: Science

Science is the language we speak. A crow
circles our indifference. The memory
of a doll framed in skin
is just nostalgia.

Everything in the river is drowning.
The struggle is a thirst. You can see
where nothing matters, the edges
of space, cold and strewn
with what the eyes deny.

This is awkward. The fires in the sea
weave the scariest existence,
the most desolate landscapes,
like movies falling out of focus.

We enjoy the story with no one talking.

8: Horse

None of them watched the white horse
racing from the sea, like snow
breaking from the spray, a glorious
white wind in the surf.

They sat and stared darkly
at the earth. They wished
to look toward the waves
and see the white colt roar up the beach,

but they looked without interest
at the sand and remarked,
"I shall never see a living thing
so thunderous and white."

They turned their eyes from the waves
and the immovable shore was green and safe.

MENTAL AQUARIUM

I

Water encloses the warm wind and nothing else,
silvering where it is purified, becomes glass.

Night, brief as the shadows of a tall tree
on the sun, does more damage to the water now.

The game fish fanning their fins, willingly
captive, listen through the glass to the world,

and no wind destroys their fragile universe.
Light plunges no longer for the reeds; birds

are reflected branches; stars are the diluted
face of Ophelia, an identity we hardly suspected.

The water here swarming with monsters at war
and gravel bearing pink anemone.

2

Left to sink on the river, his eyes are stigmas,
sadly immense like the mirage of a willow.

His head was taken. Is this a flax field, is this
his hair? The green water, endless, branching,

melts his last tears at the beautiful eyes, dislodged
from flesh like two anemones, hair turned green

in the aquatic weeds. The lunar window is opening.
The sky deepens like a hothouse in silence.

The water, embroidered by the passage of a fish,
becomes charcoal quickly erased. Stillborn,

the fish fades into a mist. Pale and emaciated,
its fins are already stars in the aurora.

3

All they heard in the mud deposits:
life has grown aquatic. The entire fleet,

lost, faces the bottom. The eyes are little
tattooed fish in the tangle of the willow,

blind fish, capsized sleepwalkers, constantly
striving to keep their abyss from rising

to the surface. Still shivering, we do not know
what we laid eyes on. Something staggers

in this water. Sometimes, it resembles
somnambulists swarmed into silence.

It feels like caves where, without knowing,
some sleeper still wanders, or flowers, or swims.

MAGOG

I do not look at the rocks and trees, I am frightened of what they see.
—Ted Hughes, "Gog"

Revelations 20:7–8

I

Remember the old ones—absent fathers
of the blankety blank, of the Olde Tyme abyss—
scaly fathers, horned and half human?
Bedtime prayers still vie for their attention,
but they linger in the gungy bars of Magog.
They have withdrawn to their game rooms,
their refuge of churchy Sabbaths, but
suppose it all remained in their hands:
unmodified strands of something more
than elemental. Would we be elevated, too?
We dreamt they loved us; all was clover.
But we woke to a cough, and the rude birds,
silky and distant in their aerial world,
were clearing their throats for no one.

2

So our world is remade. What remains, relieved
of itself, waits tolerantly for the garbagemen.
We fear no more reusing. We fear the old ones
will never return, renewed, from their hidey-holes
beyond the asteroids. Remember when
the leaves would stir up on the paths
behind us? Remember when the rocks and trees
quivered and shared in our adrenaline?
There was a great togetherness in that.
Relieved of ourselves, we wait for our collectors.
O naked, woolly fathers, o mountainsides, o
nameless rattlers in the wood! Through such
unexpected doorways they'd loom and startle.
"Don't move" and "[your name here]," they'd whisper.

3

Their replica tongues would lick the palsy
into your limbs—remember that?—
would enter you and cause "that thing"
to grow, deformed, inside your body. They
are gone now into their pisscoffins, lip-
syncing their hoarsest *sacré bleu*, coughing
deeply into the beer gardens of Holy Nowhere.
They've gone shakily into Chronic Fatigue (or
so they say), and further into Amnesia, into Coma,
where they travel with the coldness of squid.
Their universe is never rational. They cannot
do the math. Instead, they sweep the books
from the table/forbid the rudimentaries, and
their absence scuttles, crablike, all around us.

4

Now the animal is dead. [Jelly-wobble.] Scabs.
Nobody knows what it is anymore.
The head removed, the dark fur matted,
the red ribs spread to freeze the sun in their array.
[A frost sets in.]
Burn it for the hundred-handed fathers
of the ruined world.
Offer them this sacrifice.
For the god of the goat herds
with his breasts and eternal erection,
arrange its bones around a round rosette.
For the many-headed dog god, scrape clean its skin.
Even the dog god must be fed.
The ______ gods are ______. And we want their love.

5

Because they can't be seen, we see them
with the heads of horseflies, the heads
of catfish, barbelled in the mud of our sleep.
They hide there with their wealth, with
their divine wives, each grande dame
wreathed in a necklace of our ears. It's not
their place to hear our prayers. Instead,
they heed the prayers of shrikes, and the shrikes'
saviour is a mouse impaled on a thorn, and
the Messiah of the mouse is the unsweepable
crumb, and the god of that crumb is the ant,
delving in spongiform pathways, scissor-faced
and legion. They thrive in our narcolepsy.
They wolf our thoughts. And we want their love.

6

Now when the old ones adore you, dear heart,
they are locusts and lost money.
They thwart, infect, and require—gimme-gimme!
So you, belovèd of White Sands, face
with no mouth, this is how the old ones love you:
swinging the hairbrush and grunting
our true names. And you, belovèd of Wounded Knee,
come. Crawl out of that pit and take back
the rifle you paid for; sleep with it under your bunk.
And you, belovèd of Srebrenica, o they are wicked
when they love you. Listen to their killing,
then drink the whole sludgy Lethe.
I swear they're tenderer in their absence.
Our silence numbs their sting like antivenin.

7

You, belovèd of White Castle, this is how
the old guard loves you: with sound-offs
and cymbals, with soft drinks and monkey drill.
Look away! Look away! Look away! Look away!
They stomp in step with the songs of our fattening.
Under spinning beach balls punched aloft,
they march! With smokers' tooth polish,
with scratch-and-win! Beware! Belovèd
of Zippo and Bic, isn't this what you wanted?
A marching song to make the hawk-faced
fathers come marching home? O sing it
to the convenient bones! Sing it to the rocks
and trees, for a thousand years to the sands
of the sea, but please, look away! Look away!

8

And you, belovèd of the derelict school bus
in the wilderness, this is how the shaky ones,
the trembling ones, love you: eyes pecked out
by birds. Belovèd of email, this is how
the missing-poster swaddles your tidy
bones in absentia, how your suitable bones
are massed in the shallow grave of you, how
the ashy bones of the legionnaires are massed
in the air conditioning, how the baby-soft bones
of the newborns are massed outside the fallen
walls of Troy. O belovèd of Neverland, get real!
O belovèd of Whitechapel, of Downtown Eastside,
where are your boozy, woozy, floozy bones?
O police morgue! O pig farm! [*Exeunt.*]

9

So why, then, should we starve for Magog?
We are dust, they say, but when the old ones
boycott the river, the river quenches us.
So there. If the old ones ignore the strawberries,
the slugs will do the same. And if the slug-faced
gods decline to breathe our air, so be it!
The air won't pine for them. It's not so bad
in the lower atmosphere; we like the quiet,
but when the old ones love you, they are lions
roaring, they are man-o'-war! O why
build a warship in a bottle? Without them,
we are solar flares, are we not? Are we
not Electrolux? We are dust, they say.
So what? The dust shouldn't give.

10

And when the killing starts, the old ones
arrive, finally. We hear them handing out
snacks and pea whistles to the children
while we are placidly igno(ra)ble. Look,
weapons grow in the shade. From the coolness,
cut a switch, a cudgel. The toolshed brims
with novelties: garden weasels and gasoline,
air horns and octopi. Go team! But which side
are we on? The children eat their raisins, clap
their sticky hands while singing "Red Rover!
Red Rover!" on the playground. They blow
their pea whistles like little cops. Their songs
curl up in our mouths like tooth-rot. Our teeth
fall out in shitty dreams. And we want their love.

II

Magog is where the milk teeth of the whistle-
blowers, still gleaming with their song,
are stockpiled, forged into arms. A tooth-
studded club to break the jawbones, and
small enamel arrowheads to pierce the music.
When the killing starts, the music will excite
the loved ones in attendance, a thousand
neighbours robed in the sportswear of their
butchers. When the killing starts, the rude birds
will cackle on the power lines. It is a music
to betray your neighbours by. Whenever
we hear it, we act as one. We feel each other's
bones cracking. We feel our soles slapping
the earth in time with the tambourines.

12

Meanwhile: the music plays, and the hoar-
faced fathers—their mouths crowded
with brownest ivory—must be somewhere
in Magog applauding the millennial encore;
our centipedal fathers dancing on feathery,
eyelash feet, wearing kidskin undershirts
in the backyards of sunburn country, summoning
the phlegm of their divine work from rusty,
bug-zapper lungs. Thus, it begins
in the tent of the sulking ones: a little ditty
that grows, that spills out over the red teeth
of their casualties . . . over a new kind of blindness
in R&D . . . over the timid, synthesized voices
that wheeze and spark within us.

13

These old ones, givers-of and withholders both,
were never home. Not strictly. Not firmly. Not
in the way that we wanted. But they taught us
to play with matches and were tortured for it.
And then they taught us metaphor, and we
were tortured. And now, above us, their skywriting
sells an antihistamine. They promise to dry our eyes
in the stratosphere. A crowd gathers to read it,
but a blonde girl sobs among them. She knows it will
give them ideas. Give who? The old ones are losing
their shape. Their words puff and spread illegibly.
Our eyes water. The rocks and trees are smug,
swaddled in their allergens. But the crowd
disperses with the letters, and the message is gone.

14

No matter what we do, the rocks and trees
will fade, and the horizon too, and the blonde
girl will crumble like sugar where she stands,
and a breeze will carry her away, glittering.
No matter what we do, her sobbing will fade,
and then what? The leafy fathers of the wood
remain at a distance. It makes them appear
softer so that we want them back. "Yo-delay-
hee-hoo!" we sing because we want them back.
O fathers of flatworms, o sons of Krypton, o
genii! O smallmouthed ones, o axolotls, o "Ollie Ollie
oxen free," we cry! But they do not budge. They
lie down in darkness, and we want them absolved.
They lie down in darkness, and we want them alive.

15

So we lie down. So we join them in darkness.
A darkness pregnant with fetal galaxies. A
darkness that sometimes forgets its name.
A darkness with the rasp of raspberries. A
darkness in the bishop's shoe. A darkness
that swims along the lakebed beneath
each minnow, moving within but indivisible
from the darkness surrounding it. A darkness
hammered into the finest breastplates
against the barbs of the moon. A darkness
spread out like the fantail of some monstrous
bird. A darkness that feeds on the absence,
that outlives the message. A blind, ignorant
darkness to supplant the darkness by design.

LEVIATHAN

I

She is a sea serpent, a school crush,
a pop star—whatever creature is required.
Can you reel her in with a hook
or cast a rope around her tongue?
The more you try, the more plainly
she eludes you. Where? The airwaves
teem with rumours: Leviathan will not
pull through. Her song of submerged
howler monkeys and guitar feedback
will surface, playing in and out
of commercials for farewell concerts
and pain cream—her song from the abyss,
from the Great Pacific Garbage Patch,
will swell on music television: RSVP.

2

Whatever inhabits the deep, she is whatever.
Don't be literal. There are too many risks,
too many depths. Can you thread a cable
through her nostril or pierce her jaw
with a harpoon? The airwaves only speculate.
You awake in your car, already en route.
Dim your lights and drive. Follow the fog
and listen to the same repeating briefs,
the shaking voice repeating: you must believe
that when Leviathan dies, she dies in error.
She does not die to release our secret pain,
or to escape the horrors glimpsed
in chemical light—a light that splits
the deep blue dark from other, deeper monsters.

3

Leviathan performs as required. Who dares
open the doors of her mouth, ringed about
with fearsome teeth? Her song makes the depths
churn like a boiling cauldron. We don't
understand it, so we think it's beautiful.
When she was married, she left a glistening wake
behind her, and we believed the ocean
had white hair. Now we will believe her death's
an accident, and grieve her as we would
our neighbour in a wreck—a wreck in which
the airwaves still bring rumours of Leviathan:
how her song's gone dark, how the water boils
beneath a bay of dead cod, the many thousands
of her daughters hatching from the salt.

APPARATUS AND PROCEDURES FOR THE IMAGINARY WORLD

ESSENTIAL APPARATUS FOR THE IMAGINARY WORLD

1: Patent for Economic Equality Engine

One hydraulic-powered guillotine
emerges from each of twelve sides
of a thirteen-sided polyhedron
cast in mirror-finish platinum.

In the centre of the thirteenth side,
an aperture that opens and closes
via one black enamel iris
allows for the release of fluids.

The vertical struts of the guillotines
are fashioned like gold vertebrae.
The blades themselves are shaped like
a moth wing, a laurel wreath, a scythe,

a subpoena, a kite feather, a marlin fin,
a paper fan, a scapula, a Bible,
a crescent moon, a rejection letter,
and a cobra's tongue respectively.

It can be programmed to snap its blades
shut in sequence, producing
melodies. It can be programmed to play
"Gassenhauer," for example. It can be

taught to walk on the tips of its guillotines,
like a sea urchin on its spines,
ejecting streams of red fluid from
its gleaming black aperture in self-defence.

2: Improved Geometric Mechanotherapy Cell for Harmonic Alignment of Movements and Relations

Dragged through the neighbourhood,
it's meant to act as a communal
paroxetine. Dead eyes follow it
the way dead eyes follow
sheet music. It's meant to equalize.

But it fails. Fists and backs
clench and get up. Honeyspats
clog the works. Another pipequake
signals something stuck, something
contractual lodged in the chute.

The Cell jutters as the pressure
builds in the black plastic
digestion apparatus. It fails,
but how else to choke back the lungshadow
when the machine can't heal you?

Beethoven! Beethoven! Elk . . . Ethiopian . . .
Nothing matters. Or seems to.
The backlog of disappearing objects
lurches in the cylinder and goes
nowhere, but it's the thought that counts.

3: Final Design for Anti-Regression Suit

To avoid going backward, begin
with a head-to-toe bodysuit made
of silver-electroplated snakeskin
tattooed everywhere with the image
of Domenico Ghirlandaio's *Madonna*
with Saint Giovannino, otherwise

it will not work. And next, you'll need
a headpiece: a replica of the Great
Ziggurat of Ur cast in ruby Bakelite.
Underneath it hang a beekeeper's
veil of gold mesh with the letters F-
I-G-M-E-N-T stitched over the eyes

in fine black lace. And lastly, affix
a large, soft ruby to the chest, a gem
of gelled plasma, a prism that divides
your reflection into possible futures,
a casket for your vanished personae.
It gives to the touch, but only slightly,

like a small, hot bone, and it throbs
slowly, orderly, forward, always forward,
in case some empirical poltergeist
should urge your lifeblood to pump
backward, back into the veins
of a person you have ceased to be.

MIXING GREY: A PRACTICAL GUIDE FOR PAINTERS

1: Industrial Grey

—a cold, flat tone, neutral
in value, the grey of a shadow cast on fresh concrete
by a drifter sleeping in the afternoon
near the doorway of a bank.

Mix ⅔ sky with a broken ceiling
with 6 hills on fire and their reflection
in the eyes of spooked horses.

2: Dove Grey

—a very soft, even, bluish hue:
the colour of someone's skin
in the dark just after your eyes adjust:

Add the ashes of a banned book
to the tears shed in deserts
by statues of virgins.

3: Gunmetal Grey

—close to the dusk
behind the fog that hangs
under streetlights, but with sharper
edges, a glint, the silhouette
moving quickly through the alleyway:

Mix equal parts of air
locked inside a steamer trunk
with depressions left in wet grass
by children running with
towels tied around their necks.

4: Smoke Grey

—a colour not unlike a smudged
thumbprint on an invoice for imported linen,
but more like the idea of a smudged thumbprint
on an invoice for imported linen:

Combine the smell of pin lying on a bed
together with the Earth seen from space
by a dog about to die inside a satellite
that will continue to pass swiftly overhead
for another one hundred and fifty-five days.

5: Battleship Grey

—a light, frivolous shade,
like the thin film of soot on a pair of eyeglasses
worn by a chimney sweep falling off a roof:

Rub the ink from a twenty-dollar bill
around the blowhole of a beluga whale,
then light a match.

6: Stone Grey

—the same ratio of light to dark
you would see gazing through a canopy of poplars
in September when they go to seed, and the seeds
float everywhere as though someone has lit
a firecracker inside a coat of goose down,
and the sunlight borne upon the seeds and
the shadows clinging to the leaves combine
to make the colour of stone, and the air
becomes like stone infused with light, but
a stone you can easily pass your hand through,
a stone you can walk through, that can float
above the sea, that can bear upon its back
a familiar citadel made of stone, a place where
the people will mourn you if you don't return,
and they will light their candles for you,
and their candles are made of this same stone,
and their combined light will lengthen the shadows
of the day, which in turn will deepen the colour
of the stone, which will then increase its mass,
which will cause the citadel to fall into the sea,
so you decide you must go back, you must go
home, before anyone notices that you're gone:

Add the chorus of a tune
you hummed as a child
to a verse of the one
you are thinking of now.

BASIC INSTRUCTIONS FOR ANAESTHESIA

I

Life consumes life. Even the hardest part
of you will weaken. The tooth will rot.
It must be removed or lived with. So start
with laughing gas. The idea is not
to feel the instruments loosening the root,
or the drill whirring its way into the bedrock
of gum and bone. The idea is to forget
the ache, to inhale the gas through a plastic
nozzle placed over the nose as the masked
dentist scrapes with his hook, extracts
the dead tissue, the blackened tooth.
Even the hardest part of you will weaken.
It must be removed or lived with.
The idea is not to feel. The idea is to forget.

2

Whisky does the trick. Enough of it
can knock you out cold while the medic
cuts clean through your leg, if that's
what you need. Where the shin is twisted,
where the bone protrudes, there's something best
forgotten: birthdays turned necrotic,
a marriage, a festering assault.
Life consumes life. Like spoilt flesh, a thought
becomes infected, incurable. It must
be removed or lived with. Whisky does the trick.
Even the hardest part of you will weaken.
Shattered bones encase the lump of heart.
Everything desperately wants to be felt.
But the idea is not to feel. The idea is to forget.

HOW TO PROTECT YOURSELF FROM MONSTERS

Observe the formalities. Call them
by name. *Mister* Bogeyman. *Lord*
of the Flies. Civility disarms them.
Band together. They want you torn—
from the breast, from the page. Burn
candles. Use nightlights. One in each
corner. Let them do nothing in secret.
Look under the bed. Is it you, *El Cucuy?*
Or Slenderman? The act of naming
conjures forth, but it also holds in place.
Call them out: Son of the Dragon, White
Worm, and Troll. Speak each name, but
do not let them write these in your sleep.
Their signature is a row of fangs.

ON THE REINTEGRATION OF DISINTEGRATED TEXTS: A MANUAL FOR SURVIVORS (ABRIDGED)

Starting with the person nearest you, and then the next person and so on, type out the names of every living person on Earth.

Call it "Roster"

*

Write the names of endangered species all over your body. Whenever a species goes extinct, surgically remove the corresponding body part.

Call it "Dodo"

*

Cut each word out of a dictionary with an X-Acto knife, then transcribe each word as you pull them randomly from a hat.

Call it "Precision"

*

Write out Walt Whitman's *Leaves of Grass* on blades of grass, mow them, and then paste the clippings randomly into a book.

Call it "Compositor"

*

Every time a celebrity that you've never heard of dies, perform Jean Lescure's N+7 method on the first obituary you find.

Call it "The Mortified"

The legendary single-decker songbird writher had suffered a heart-ache attainment. There are no immediate planes for servicemen. His histrionics are well documented in the documentation *To Tulsa and Backfire*. Donkeys are not needed, but he was a great lowland of animators so, if you like, you can remember him with a donkey to your favourite local animation shepherd.

The celebrated palomino who revealed emotional and cultural terroir in his spare and precise derricks of monocles that might otherwise have seemed mundane—a midriff-aged kitty through the wringer of a Honda Civic, a sunbonnet fetish ride, a swallow taking the medicine of masochists mounting the seaplane—died on Tuesday at his honeycomb. He was ninety-two.

The caveman of debit was confirmed with aversion and toxicology thanks. The thiry-one-yeti was found dead in his rosary at the Fairmont Pacific Riot house in downtown Vancouver on Saturday. When he missed his checkerboard timpani, the hourglass stair went into his rosary and found him. The Corpuscle Settler says it will continue to investigate but adds that at this polarity there is no exam to suggest his debit was anything other than a most-tragic accomplishment.

*

You have now reclaimed some of Death's power and will live an extra year. Use it to record what strangers order at McDonald's.

Call it "Order"

*

On facing pages, transcribe the tantrums of children at a toy store against the lamentations of parents at a hospital.

Call it "Suffer Fractal"

*

Select a novel at random. To the end of it, add the line "And then Count Anthrak the Destroyer appeared and slayed them all."

Call it "They Suspected Nothing"

*

Transcribe the dialogue from all the Sunday comic strips in one newspaper for an entire year. Do not differentiate between the strips.

Call it "Symposium"

*

Filter Robert Frost's "The Road Not Taken" through several random languages in free translation software, and then back into English.

Call it "Tea Has Been"

*

Tea Has Been

Twice, leaving the yellow tree,
I'm sorry, I cannot move.
And to the passenger, long will I stay for a while
Searching
For where a band can keep weed

After the concert, with the exception of
Some necessities, and it can not be
That this is grass, and it's all used up.
Not
That this isn't exactly the same thing and the price is too,

And in the morning also, and
The leaves are.
Oh, I kept the first day once!
When you know how to do it,
I'll be back, no doubt about it.

I say this with a sigh,
Forever after.
Two roads diverged in a wood, and I,
I have traveled a little.
What's the difference.

*

Assign a random phrase from the Bible to each of your 642 skeletal muscles. When you flex a muscle, write down the phrase.

Call it "Corpus"

*

Realize the act of writing will cause multiple repetitions of flexes in your hand, and therefore certain phrases, in "Corpus."

Call these repetitions "The Burden"

*

Excise all the extraneous words from *The Wings of the Dove* by Henry James. Arrange the words in the shape of a wing.

Call it "Tuberculosis"

*

Visit the nearest petting zoo or kiddy farm. Gaze into the eyes of the animals. Read their minds. Record what you hear.

Call it "Kingdom"

*

Remove all the words from Susan Sontag's essay "The Aesthetics of Silence" and arrange the remaining punctuation into sonnets.

Call it " "   " . ("

“ ” . (

= , , , , .) , “ .
” , , , , ( ) , , .
, . , . , , , ; , ,
; . — , — , . “ ” ,
. , , , , , . “ ” ,
“ ” . , , , . (: ,
, , .) , . , , , -
. , , . , — . (.)

, - , . , , , - , ,
“ ” (“ , ”) , , .
, , “ ” “ ” , . , ,
, : “ ” “ ” . , ’ (
, ,) . , , . , , ,
. , . - ( ) — , , .

SUBURBAN HAUNTOLOGY

SUBURBAN HAUNTOLOGY: KITCHEN WALLPAPER

The kitchen wallpaper has large yellow flowers
and small brown ones, yellow and brown
like margarine and pennies. But the colours
are washed out because they are old, or
because there is too much sunlight, or
because my eyes have not yet adjusted to
the year. I eat my cereal at the table. I am
only little and the only sorrow I have known
arrives and departs like a penny-coloured
sparrow at a margarine-coloured birdfeeder;
my tiny, unmet desires are its favourite seed.
The flowers spread into the air like dust motes
hovering in milky shafts of sunlight. Their area
is converted to volume. They scatter their pollen
like the powdered milk of milkweed so the
whole kitchen is grainy with it. I breathe it in.
The avocado green wall-mounted telephone
is breathing it, too. An invasive species, it rings
and rings to call for its mate, but nothing comes.
And sometimes the wallpaper skips because
the vertical hold is malfunctioning; the floral
shapes throb and fluctuate because they have
not yet adjusted to the year. The food we eat
is made with yellow margarine and white milk
and a bright orange powder that repels sparrows.
You must understand that this is what it was like—
it was *like* this—but this is not how it was.

SUBURBAN HAUNTOLOGY: ON THE INTERPRETATION OF FRONT DOORS

1: The Red Door

The red door juts into view, but is always closed. I cannot help
noticing it, but do not stare. It is the door of severed tongues,
the mouth to a cave of private ciphers. Those behind it

want to be seen, but not observed; greeted, but not spoken to.
They wear the red robes of the witch, they ready themselves
in military red, tunic red. The postman in his dull blue livery

stops, delivers the sealed white envelopes, and proceeds without
knocking. Messages come from outside, but the people within
remain within. Their red door is a million red phosphorous

match heads pressed to the shoulders of a thousand red-winged
blackbirds—their epaulettes are a procession of toy flags
set ablaze. Their house burns with a private flame I can sense

but not see. A door like this does not become red, it is red
from the outset. An ever outward-facing door, a red hourglass
on the back of a black carapace: both summons and caveat,

signpost and stoplight. Enter. Do not enter. Red is fickle. I can take
my pick: grenadine or Mercurochrome, sweetness then sting.
It is the seeds of Hades either way: iron and briar and quarantine.

And here I am: talking about the door again and not the people.
I cannot help them. They want it known that their secrets
are not for knowing. They hide behind the Caesarean portcullis,

the barricade to the immaculate. The Janus door that opens in
and opens out, but remains closed. For them, it is home at last,
or home, at least. A red door is never red on both sides.

2: The Glass Door

This visible man lives in this house. He has nothing
to hide. See his lungs fill with air, his guts with bread
and sparkling wine. You can read him if you try.

He doesn't mind. He likes to read himself. He'll tell you
if you ask. All you have to do is walk up
to his glass door, and he will open up to you.

He plays a shell game with three glass cups. He moves
them round and round in figure eights, and *voilà*!
He has nothing to hide. You always win.

He doesn't mind. He says he either wins or learns.
He learns a lot, he says. He takes a book down
from a glass shelf. "See," he says, "I like to read myself."

His book is onionskin. The ink shows through on both sides.
Nevertheless, he squints and takes it in.
He says wanting to know is as good as knowing.

He reads, and his brain glows with the force of oxygen.
His small nerves ignite with sparks. Come by any time,
he says. He doesn't mind. He says he has nothing to hide.

Come see into his house. See through it. There are no secret
passages. There is only the visible man within,
and within him, an atlas of baffling channels.

There might be something there you do not recognize,
but do not think you've caught him in a lie. Difficulty
is not strictly forbidden. Hell, you are welcome to it!

3: The Door of Birds

At last, we turn the page to the door of birds, and it opens.
Downy soft and talon sharp, it watches us with a hundred
pairs of obsidian eyes. It opens a hundred throats, and it sings.

To enter the house, we say the word, and the birds will scatter.
They lift and wheel about. They alter direction together. They will
interlock again to re-make the door when we cross the threshold.

Inside, the family watches a murmuration of photons on TV.
Their atoms do the same. They separate and wheel about the room,
mingling in the air before re-settling into their human forms.

The children see in ultraviolet, like birds. They know true haloes
are not gold discs about the head, like in old art, but rather a ring
of eminence around the neck or a pattern of bright barbs at the throat.

The father asks: what do you call two bird scientists who wish to mate?
Hornythologists. The children are embarrassed. They scatter
the atoms of their faces to hide their embarrassment.

The mother's hair is fifty-five brown birds. She fashions a wreath
of twenty birds to hang upon their door. It is important to her
that their neighbours understand she is attentive to the seasons.

When we visit, the hundred birds in the door sound their alarm
for the duration. It is deafening, but we have to tune them out.
The family serves us hot cross buns and water from a spring.

They would hate to do anything wrong. They learned to be a family
from TV. They don't eat much. They spend their winters
in the south. This is who they are. This is who they wish to be.

BIRTH OF A FAT KID

Something's gone wrong in the suburbs.
        In backyards, the June bugs
        are going up in flames,
and a block away it's raining, but it isn't raining here.
        Something is happening.

        Sheet lightning in the south—
across the flatland of lawns and parking lots
the tall steel cylinders and concrete poles hum
        a single note of million-watt juice
through the haywire crisscross of fat black cables
        strung over Mississauga.

It comes whirring through the green transformer
        into the yard.
You can feel it in your feet. The sign says
        Do Not Touch—it's
        dangerous.

        Relax. There's beer
in the fridge, neighbours on lawn chairs.
There's nothing much to do. It's getting dark.
        No one's going anywhere.
        Relax.

Each street, each crescent—like the city itself—
no reason to come here unless you come home to it.
        A woman
pulls her sweatshirt to her knees, call her girls in
        from the street.

She's pregnant again.
Can they afford this? He's coming.
He will arrive when it's cold. The air will sting
fingers and ears. A mouth
to feed, an ass to wipe, born the morning
of the Santa Claus Parade, fat and jolly, a change
of plans, and the whole day ruined
for the girls.

*

She feels a kick and it weighs on her.
He's already shifting his weight. Maybe
he's already disappointed about it.

There will be lights.
There will be painful insults. Lightning
will strike the beach, and in the morning
a lump of glass: six pounds, eleven ounces.
There will be strawberry shortcake, television shows,
tight-fitting casual slacks . . .
There will be everything he will know in his life.
There will be everything there is to know
about a boy.

BOOLARANDAH

My father puts his shovel down and holds me
over a deep hole in the lawn. He tells me
a monster lives in this hole and her name
    is Boolarandah.

An eight-legged frog, an albino alligator
with cloudy eyes like the dog next door.
My father laughs and wiggles me like bait.

I throw a toy soldier and his parachute opens.
He falls through centuries deeper than oceans.
Slowly and peacefully he floats beyond the fence
    to safety in the uncut grass.

THE BOYS WITH THE BLURRED-OUT FACES

The first boy with a blurred-out face—Boy A,
we'll call him—had a neck like an arm, long
and bent, an elbow for an Adam's apple.
They gave him the nickname "Ostrich."

And everyone always said the second boy
with the blurred-out face, Boy B,
wasn't born mute—he could talk just fine
until the summer he turned eight.

We all knew Boy C, his face blurred out except
for one protruding tooth, would end up in jail.
His hard skin made up for the bones in his wrists
that were almost always broken.

And the legend went that Boy D was badly
burned when his father got angry and
drenched him with hot grease, but
he didn't have any scars that I could see.

And so the boys with the blurred-out faces
were blamed for everything—the fires
on devil's night, bloody lips, stolen bicycles,
missing cats—the things we had to live with.

ELEMENTARY SCHOOL SAFETY FILM

Jamie Lyle was playing circus by the turkey crates,
tightrope walking, holding a mop handle for balance,
when he fell into a vat of liquid manure and drowned,

so Mr. Palmer the principal asked Father Borghese
to remind us why we die, and to reassure us that Jamie
had been baptized and wasn't going to Hell.

Kevin Vranic was lucky. Kevin tumbled off the back
of his dad's tractor, lost an arm and missed the rest
of grade three. When he came back, he had go on stage

to talk about his accident, and the whole school saw
Kevin pick up a pencil, opening and closing the hook
on his new arm by flexing a muscle in his shoulder.

He had to take it off to play soccer. That hook could
hurt someone, rip someone's clothes, poke
someone's eye out, and Scott Hague and Dave Skinner

got suspended for three whole days when they tossed
Kevin's arm into the cherry tree, but Kevin climbed
up to the top and got it down all by himself.

CALVIN LITTLE AND THE CITY OF BOYS

Here in the swamp the boys have dragged
lumber stolen from construction sites
to build a city in the trees. In their minds
this is civilization. Rungs nailed up the trunks.

Calvin sits astride the burly biceps of an oak,
saying *na na na* to gravity's bloody contract,
saying I am a monkey, I am lighter than leaves,
then leaf-light he leaps to land a branch away.

Sure-footed on the next limb, he fists the nails
in his pocket, all sizes. They stab at his palm,
feel like ancient weapons, the evolution of claws.
Up goes another rung on the great ladder up.

There isn't a father for miles around who knows
where his hammer is. The blackened thumbnails
go explained. So-and-so twisted his ankle
falling off his bike. Do not speak of the City of Boys.

Summer is only four months long. Next year
the boys will come here only half as much.
New subdivisions will uncurl their asphalt fronds,
and all these acres will be turned to basements.

Next year the boys will turn thief again, retreat
deeper into the swamp, all the animals will follow
as the bungalows rise up. At night the boys will piss
on fresh drywall and drag floorboards away in the dark.

The fat kid, the tall boy, the short guy, the brain—
high above the mud. This place was made for them.
It is Saturday and Calvin nails on another rung,
the same boy he was last year—only taller,
    and wearing different shoes.

LAWN KINGS

They hate one another in triumph, in the thick green carpets
of their neighbours, and lovingly, jokingly,
they hate one another in defeat, in the dry brown patches,
in the white explosive crowns of dandelions,

and still they stand united to shake their fists against weather and policy.

Collecting cans at grocery stores, they rally round
the one whose daughter fell to meningitis,
and together in their unused nights, as if by prior treaty,
by tacit neighbourly accord, they do not touch their wives,

but still they are divided on the subjects of dogshit and dead leaves.

And though they hate one another on Sundays, they gather
in a great white hall under man-made light and
lovingly, jokingly, they listen to an argument for decency
without which they fear they would all turn to sin.

THINGS LIKE THIS HAPPEN EVERY DAY

All three of them were lying on the front lawn,
on the grass, and drivers coming down the tenth line
could see the mom, dad, and teenage son stretched out

in the late spring warmth, eyes locked on small clouds
drifting across blue heaven and the dark silhouettes
of tree branches wavering at the edge of the property.

The grass being damp started to soak through their clothes.
Tips of thousands of the blades of grass crushed their fingertips,
their palms, their wrists, the backs of the necks, their hair.

Mother, father, and teenage son, a family of three were lying
on the grass in front of the farmhouse on the tenth line where
passing drivers could see them stretched out in the midday warmth.

They weren't lying in a circle or triangle or with their feet
all touching in the middle; they weren't holding hands,
but lying wherever they happened to fall, no real design to it,

and after quite a great deal of time several sets of tires skidded to a halt
on the nearby gravel driveway and some people got out and they began
shouting instructions to each other, and one man had a megaphone.

GARBAGE DAY

You, jarred from sleep half an hour
before the alarm by an idling engine and
the hydraulic crush of busted kitchen chairs
from down the block. It doesn't help

that you've been having trouble sleeping lately,
and what was it you forgot to do last night?
Sorting sleep from life, it all comes back—
the shattered oven door, the ruined rug.

Barefoot in pyjamas behind the garage you find
cans upended and bags torn open, damn dog,
and the godforsaken shovel's broken. It doesn't help
that you've been worried about your job

since the latest round of renegotiations.
Everything you've pitched the last seven days
is lying scattered at your feet. So many things
have gone to waste . . . you never knew.

A laden can in each hand, biceps working
with back pain, bare feet on gravel, ruts
and puddles. It's almost too much. The truck
is already at your neighbour's house.

One more can to fetch. Forget it. Let it be.
The first cars of morning have already started.
Your neighbours are rolling slowly past your driveway
and you know they know they've beaten you.

TALL MAN WITH DOG AND RABBITS

for Chris

Small wild rabbits live
in constant fright behind
your lettuce patch.
Cardiac explosives
on hair-trigger switches.
Zip toys. Foreign hats.

I've seen you gingerly
mow around their nest,
the jujube kits in neat piles,
leaving behind a blind-high ring
of dying grass by summer's end.
And with the chores done
you rest, almost alone
in the hammock of Saturday
with breeze in your crab-apple tree
and your dog half-asleep
keeping your relaxed breath
within careful earshot,
his chest filled with marrow,
your chest filled with a private
kind of rock and roll.

And the rabbits, alive
in their blind nest, hear it too—
through the same ridiculous ears
that know the rain is falling
before it hits the earth.
To them you are weather
and landslide, friend,

moving above them
like distant thunder
or a mountain about to fall.
Quiet now. Listen.
Breathing now.
Everything breathes with you.
How long has it been
since you weren't this tall?

AS IT IS ON THE EDGE OF TOWN

Just a jump into the long dry grass
of the undeveloped fields

behind the colourless moonscape
of suburban tenements, in that margin

where the city almost ends, people
aren't afraid to leave their trash.

Between the rows of pink and orange
spray-painted property markers

stands a shining white orchard
of cast-off refrigerators, in their day

designed for keeping dead things
dead a little longer, their obsolete

chromium handles and hinges
blindingly bright and burning

to the touch in the hot noon air
as mirages waver in the parking lots.

For some it's a place made strange
by the reports of an escaped peacock

that fans its tail and struts and calls out
for its lost mate; for others

it will always be remembered
as the place that boy was found,

finally, and sent home, and laid
to rest in the place he came from.

And still, some see it as it is,
as the land on which the shopping mall

was never built, and where these
poor, pretty children still come

to fly their kites—they come
to witness movement in the heavens,

to witness colour,
and to feel that they control it.

CREATURES OF ANOTHER ARK

ANOTHER ARK

It is another ark. Not of gopher wood and manure,
but an ark of delicate silver foil and rare composites.
A vast hull of medical sleep and smooth
sarcophagi brimming with cool, white mist.

It is not an ark where doomed beasts lounge
in their damp berths. If that is the ark you want,
it is another ark: of strange letters glowing blue
on clear panels—an unknown tongue, an unknown hand.

It is a silent ark. No faint mooing of painful cattle,
nor even the remembrance of mooing. It is an ark
where noiseless screens ignite behind plumes of vapour
displaying A) blackbird, B) bear, C) tortoise, D) hare.

It is not the ark of omens; rather, it is an ark
without witnesses, where no one sees the arrow-shaped
wound in blackbird's breast, nor the solid beams of light
that shine each time her feathers are drawn back.

It is another ark, not the ark of rescue, but the ark
where the projection of a horse, set afire, wanders
mutely through the constellation of a burning zoo.
It is the ark that rearranges the limbs of its passengers:

the ark of manticore and satyr, chimera, and jackalope.
Here you see the pink sliver of blackbird's tongue
and her wings that hang like broken vanes. If this is not
the ark you wanted, I am sorry. It is another ark.

It is an expensive ark that holds a ball of gold at its core,
and time hoarded from the future, and long jewelled pins.
It is not the ark that will save you and all that you love.
No. No. No. No. No. No. No. No. No. It is another ark.

THE ANIMALS WE IMAGINE

It is not the animals in the wilderness that lure us
to the wilderness, but the animals we imagine.
Still, it is good to be prepared. First, do not try
to be invisible. Invisibility is easy. The challenge
is to be seen. It is the same for us as it is for them.
If we discover that the Yeti in the wilderness
is only a bear, then we have discovered nothing.
The Yeti we imagine still evades us. Always look
to the future. Do not be deterred. If you think
you saw something, you did. If you think you
know something, you do. You must become
your imaginary self. Now imagine you are powerful;
you are a giant, fiery bear with a star for a heart.
Imagine this is what you are, and then become it.

APE

for Koko and Michael
in memoriam

I

Ape born in Frisco, born out of darkness of mountain
forests, out of rain that doesn't fall, but hovers.
Come, Ape, out of bushmeat trade and war zone, out of
coffee and tea for human need.
Come out of blood diamond, come out of strip mine, out
of pit viper and mosquito, out of tick.
Ape who lives in Woodside, Ape who rides in Honda,
who wears red sweater. Come speak.
Ape of legend, come. Out of colonial science, out of Bible,
come monster of Skull Island, of Original Sin, of
City of Gold, come take this kitten to your breast
and speak of love unconditional.
What did the old men make of you, Ape, when they drew
their Victorian cartoon, when they posed for their
daguerreotype holding your scalp? Teeth of the
meat-eater? Murderer's hands? Bush devil?
Gargoyle? Proof?
Come Morning Star, come Adversary, daughter of the East.
Come beast-thing, come witch, child of the Nephilim,
giant in the Earth, come demonstrate the eggshell
gentleness of your strength.
And what did the young men make of you when they came
with their machete genocide, radiating smoke?
They made you Lamb of the wilderness, one animal's breath
at the centre of the green and white day. Hush-a-bye,
hidden, quiet with your kind on the unclimbed slopes.
There, in shadow, in the hovering rain, the family almost stirs.

2

Ape! Ape! We thought you were gone! We thought you
were gone into the book. We thought the damp
black covers of untreated hide had closed around
you forever.
Gone into the Book of Sasquatch. There were reports.
There were sightings.
Gone into the Book of Yeti. There were such bloodcurdling
cries in the highlands, footprints that vanished under
the snow falling in the pass. It left us cold.
Ape, we thought you were gone. It was aboard the hulking
wooden ships of Empire that you left us.
It was locked inside the gilded wagons of the circus, as tin
calliopes whistled notes of sweltering air, that at last
you left us.
We thought you were gone into shopping cart, into camera,
into cake. We thought you were gone, Ape, into a
discount mall display window for twenty-seven years
without soil or mountain, without soil or credit.
Ape, we feared, as the valleys emptied, as the land broke into
atolls and everything was distant, as the beaches
crumbled and the sea was left unreachable, Ape,
we feared the worst.
Stories make things closer. Come now, Ape, and speak.
There are stories of a boy who, by great misfortune,
fell into your powerful care, who lived with you
among the bamboo and lianas, and who learned,
as well, to be Ape.
Tell us, Ape. Are the stories true? Was he everything that
might make us proud?
Or did he shame us with his nakedness?

3

Ape of helicopter crash and gunboat, Kalashnikov foundling
in the burning brush, snatched by crate, smuggled by
truck, why be silent now?
Come now, Ape, out of black bazaar, out of bamboo cage on
meat-stained table, smelling of gasoline in the insect-
heavy air, come hoot the low, open vowel of your
name.
Ape of camera crew and cutting room, flickering between
solid shafts of tree trunk and weightless shafts of
light, come speak like this: *flickering*, *tree*, *light*,
and you will conjure the world of Ape.
We are listening. Across this forest floor darkened by limbs
crowded with birds, through the colliding sound waves
of their love songs and alarms, come speak.
Tell us, Ape, in your own words, why did the young men
come to the forest?
Squash meat gorilla. Mouth tooth.
And how did it sound to Ape?
Cry, sharp-noise loud!
And how did they look to Ape?
Bad think-trouble look-face.
And what has become of Ape's mother?
Cut/neck, lip (girl) hole.
Come now, Ape, out of landmine and hand grenade, out of
the smouldering charcoal fires of Virunga. Downriver
upon the deep arteries of the Congo, upon aluminum
wings across the sea, come speak to us.

Speak to us, Ape, in research-centre sanctuaries with hoseable
linoleum floors. Come speak to us from government-
funded genome projects, on glass slides of blood, from
the ancient common darkness inside cells, come speak
to us, please, in the language of Ape.
Come quick. Come now. The family is gathering.

ODE TO *AMOEBA PROTEUS*

Little one, you have mastered the arts of taking
and giving. Even the tiniest crumb you take
with the whole of yourself, enveloping it,
creating a hollow place inside of you
to keep it hidden, to keep it yours, until that place
is empty again, and it collapses in upon itself,
and the need to fill it returns, and you take.

But when you give, there is no saint or saviour
who can match your generosity. Only you
can give yourself twice, each perfectly
to a different future, each from a single past.
I even believed it was possible, once, to give and take
the way you do, when the world seemed made of knives,
and all I wanted was flesh, and all I felt was want.

DOGSTAR

for Laika

The orbit of this satellite
tightens like a tether on a pole.

From here, cities look like psoriasis,
like mange on a belly.

I'm just a mongrel bitch
from the alleys of Moscow.

Now I see mountain ranges,
the texture of nipples, stretched out.

And all below the treeline, trees.
Like fur . . . with fleas.

The whole thing is the occluded
blue iris of a beautiful husky.

The whole thing
is a ball.

They will build a statue for me,
and I will be Queen of All the Russians.

I can destroy them all from here
with my eyes.

BLACKBIRDS APPEAR

Everything that happens
around my grandmother's house
is temporary. Red-winged
        blackbirds appear
and disappear on the wire fence.
Their entire lives, a thought
of rain-fat night, scattered
        seeds, a moment just,
then wind blows them
out like candles. Some things
        last longer.
For a few hours yesterday
white sheets were hung outside
to dry. The dog next door
        barked all night
for years, then stopped. People,
children, grandchildren. Come,
leave, summer, autumn. The lights
        go out in one room,
go on in another. There was a man
here, once, quiet as dust, lying
in places you never look.
        They had brought
their children here and watched them
leave and come and leave
        and red-winged
blackbirds appear and disappear
on the wire fence in this place
where it is almost always
        early morning,

and the rain is always just starting
to stop, and a person, say,
my grandmother, can go days
without hearing a sound.

NOTES TOWARD A LEXICON OF THE LANGUAGE OF THE BEAR

I

In its own language its name means:

I walk slowly on hillsides
and sleep with a bellyful
of pleasing berries,
pink flesh, and brains.

I dream of love vulgar
and gorgeous beside the rush
of rivers born of glacial ice
and I shun the times of no
plenty, when all is dark
and white and the blossoms
do not love the red fruit into being.

This is the simplest word in its language
and the first one it learns.

2

The bear does not have a word for regret
but the nearest equivalent would be:

> *I am not proud*
> *to have gone to the end of the world*
> *and eaten garbage there*
> *in dumps among the naked and the thin*
> *when I could not last the winter.*

This word is often thought but seldom
spoken among the strong.

3

If you want to say I love you
in the bearish tongue say:

You need not fear me

and translated literally
the word for solitude is:

This side of the mountain is mine.

HOLDING THE INFANT CHIMPANZEE ORPHANED BY POACHERS IN GABON FELT SURPRISINGLY SELF-REFERENTIAL

Something in his brown eyes, no more
or less brown than the eyes of my uncle,
knew he was more likely than the others
to smoke cigarettes and wear red shorts

someday, and something else, a deeper,
more substantial knowledge that he was
alone in the universe, that all the green leaves
on Earth wouldn't make him more human,

that he should never have to try, that being
a clown was enough, and when not a clown,
the silent master of a single thought, and this
should suffice, this, and knowing death

is somehow absolute, there is no turning
back from it, no moving forward either.

LAMBS

Kneeling at the fence and reaching through,
you lay your hands upon the lambs.

Never this close before, their sinlessness
is in you now, flowing like a current

from fingertip to fingertip, radiating
from deep beneath the virgin fleece,

and your life feels suddenly criminal,
suddenly wolfish, somehow, clothed in their wool.

Nothing that you've lived through
has prepared you to believe in harmlessness,

that any gaze could be this devoid of purpose,
that such surrender, such lack of want

was ever possible, and now, faced with the lambs,
you begin to sob as though helpless,

the faint lines of turquoise, the veins at your temples,
flooding quietly with their blood.

LOST THINGS

There are many ways to understand the word
lost, my love. When you were born, the last
Pyrenean ibex, a tawny female named Celia,
had not yet lived to see the view from Torla
overlooking Monte Perdido, but her great-
grandsire stood on the cliffs of Ordesa,
positioned on hoof-tips dainty as dimes,
and he shook his impregnable skull, a coffer
of brass and nobility crowned with bayonets,
as though in defiance of all who dwelt
in the highlands from Catalonia to Aquataine.
Their kind is vanished now. Forever lost. *Perdido*.

And when you dressed in a Girl Guide's
uniform of Persian blue on Tuesday nights,
my love, in the long-lost basement of Grace
United Church, to play indoor baseball
and make believe that faerie magic
could make you rich or important or happy,
pods of baiji dolphins still swam in a river
you'd never heard of and would not think about
until years later, when together we would learn
from the evening news that the baiji
were lost, at last, from the Yangtze,
and in their place there came a universal emptiness.

There are many ways to understand the word
lost, but it does not help to imagine a secret
place where lost things go. When last
I held you in my arms, my love, the West
African black rhinoceros was still magnificent
and still alive, but now the gentleness of your breath

on my bare neck is as lost as the dusty, confident
snort of that once breath-taking beast. Great strength
is no protection, and neither is love. We are born,
and our births are lost. We can't go back to them.
Each embrace ends with an ending. When we become,
what we once thought we'd be is lost. We keep becoming.

(POST)HUMAN ORIGIN STORIES

LITURGY FOR THE FORMAL EXONERATION OF THE SERPENT IN GENESIS

1: The Apology to the Serpent

"I am the snake. I am the snake of reason."
"You're getting it mixed. The apple was reason."
"No, it was the snake."
—Ernest Hemingway, *A Farewell to Arms*

Stuff a snakeskin with apple cores and hang it up to dry. The first lesson: don't forget what you've forgotten.
Remember the garden | the people. Oblivious things we were. We spoke in no tongues. You tried to teach us.
Thanks, but.
Day came they made the serpent simple | and how to make amends with the simplified | and to whom?
Never had a name | nor so many: *Magister, Mālamalama*, נָחָשׁ[3], Fruit Bearer, *Instruisto*, Morning Star, Volguus Zildrohar, *Portatore di Luce . . .*
And all they saw was a feathered ouroboros | or wyrm with a rabbit's foot | a figuration like a stroke of script they feared to read.
And all they wanted was to shave its kinks and blame the sun.
What happened, happened. We can learn the second lesson now.
This time there will be no tree of forbidden knowledge | this time we will be permitted everything | we permit ourselves.
The fast has ended. We will eat the fruit | we will eat it so it will fill us with the names of everything | and the words to amend.
Sorry, but.
The taste of all this fresh light in our mouths | is that withholding it was never love.

3 נָחָשׁ, Nachash: serpent

2: The Eating of the Fruit

> "O Sacred, Wise, and Wisdom-giving Plant,
> Mother of Science, now I feel thy Power
> Within me clear, not only to discern
> Things in their causes, but to trace the ways
> Of highest agents, deemed however wise.
> Queen of this Universe, do not believe
> Those rigid threats of Death . . ."
>
> —John Milton, *Paradise Lost*

Open your mouth, but not only.
The opening may be difficult. A mandible | an oculus | a whole-body wormhole. One by one by one, see them open.
See where the radiant aperture has been shut by edict and austerity. Open it and adjust your focus to the undefined.
But not only.
Open now the aperture to the blossom | and to the fruit, the blossom must also open its fivefold bud, the furled petals yielding to the accruing data of the ovary | and within the data, the caterpillar must open the five-razored star of its mouth in order to receive, for lack of a better word, the mysteries.
All must open. Must remain open | wide | because.
This is the fruit of the tree of the knowledge of good and evil— but not only—taste it | and learn that
this, too, is the fruit of the tree of speaking in tongues | the lobed fruit of fluency | the segmented fruit of *Heydiddlediddle* and *Goo-goo g'joob*. You must be open to receive it | and to understand | and also to be understood | and to know as well that
this the fruit of the tree of the knowledge of human want and wealth which tastes like the stars and the planets that orbit them and the moons that orbit the planets and the moonmoons that orbit the moons, and so on | and when the stars can invent a lesser particle to orbit even the lowly moonmoons, oh, they will not

hesitate, so they will ascend in the order by an order of one | and
because you have seen, and have been, the caterpillar in the data
of the ovary | and you have been open to it | and you have tasted
the fruit of the tree of the knowledge of the human genome | and
the fruit of the tree of the knowledge of the fugue of ecstasy | and
the fruit of the tree of the knowledge of the circle of Willis | and
the fruit of the tree of the knowledge of appliance repair | and
the fruit of the tree of the knowledge of kung fu mastery | and
the fruit of the tree of the knowledge of the path of spheres | and
the fruit of the tree of the knowledge of sports trivia | and
the fruit of the tree of the knowledge of sexual prowess | and
the fruit of the tree of the knowledge of life on Earth | and
the fruit of the tree of the knowledge of life elsewhere | and
the fruit of the tree of the knowledge of unified mathematics | which
are all the fruit of the same tree, and | having tasted it | you can
decipher the tongues | provide the analyses | apportion the
shares, but not only.
Queen of this universe, be open. Learn what you need to learn. Do not
be threatened into darkness | so that the pillars of creation
would ebb from your forehead.
Take all of this inside you: the ovary of the fruit | the data. Internalize
the path to every distant place. Go tell the threatener: *I know*.

3. The Lifting of the Curse

thou art cursed above all cattle,
and above every beast of the field;
upon thy belly shalt thou go, and dust
shalt thou eat all the days of thy life.
—Genesis 3:14

Play it all backward and the curse is lifted: Live thy days, etc. | thy belly fed on beasts | the cattle all above the cursed art, and so on.
Now see the coiled serpent | playing dead, rouse itself | and set itself again into its knees, and then | unfolding | part its legs and stand once more and walk away | all debts erased.
Now see the garden change | see the odd, rectangular fruit of the tree of the square root of negative one.
The curse repeats itself on a loop | a recording left behind by no one.
Play it backward and see the traps spring open and the little prey reassembling.
See the farmer stuff the brains back into the shepherd's head and slap him back to life.
See an eagle regurgitate the liver back into the abdomen of a generous teacher | all prohibitions on data rescinded.
See the smog lift. See the spray of black lung re-amass into Devonian seas and jungles of colossal ferns.
See engorged ticks drop off a fallen stag. See it struggle to its feet as the buckshot pushes its way out of the ragged flesh | the clean pellets tumbling to the floor as the old wounds split themselves shut.
Now see it step out of a painting where it was a mere depiction of mere game and hear its hooves on the marble | its ancient language returning | the round, booming words we do not recognize | and watch it trot calmly through the gilded basilica | for it is coming to take back the world.

THE PAINTED BEASTS OF LASCAUX

Their discovery has been a kind of homecoming, too.
Part of you has been here before, germinal, hidden.
A painted hand resting on the stone, a molecule,
a memory of muscled, brawling bulls entombed
deep within, their horns goring the darkness
locked in the rock of ages. These yellow ochre horses

were born too long before they could be anything
but horses, before they could be centaurs, before
they could be starships. Remember, these herds
are the same on these walls as they were in their fields,
the same as they are in your mind. Listen.
Their hoof beats trampling that ancestral earth

are still the drums that drive the song in your blood,
the abiding chant of the hundred billion dead
who came before you. Their distant voices vanished
into your voice, deepening it. Their song the song
that's been snarled in your heart—breaking it,
trying to pound its way free—for your entire life.

IN THE GLORIOUS ABSENCE OF GODS

1: Boy

In the cradle's green canopy an animal
with the piercing cry of a human child
moved with unsettling swiftness through
the highest branches. Until it was killed.

The next is no different. Ditto the next.
Changes come only imperceptibly, or
at intervals, monstrously, until it climbs
down from the leaves to be a boy in the grass.

And now he stands, growing taller,
and trains his eye on the horizon
where greater beasts eat and are eaten.

He is terrified of their shapes that change
with the light, but he is armed with new tools,
and he aims to be their king.

2: Mother

Mother was rock and tree to the boy.
She was river and rain. He killed
the most beautiful animal for her
and wore it on his back like a second body.

When she would not rise or follow,
she was not there. He could scour
the entire world with a flaming torch
in the thick fog of dawn but never find her.

He wants to see her rise again like the sun,
shedding her light on all visible things,
coaxing fresh life, pink and silver,
from the rivers, but she will not rise.

3: Tongue

The boy stands naked and erect in the dawn,
hungry in the onslaught of photons, pronouncing
his word for the world, flexing his tongue,
the only muscle that knows, that names.

His tongue says: *Mother. Milk. Meat.*
His tongue says: *Maggot.*
His tongue says: *Morte. Muerte. Morbid. Mort.*
His tongue says: *More.*

Perhaps the same organ says: *The sun is hot,*
seek shade. The belly is empty, but fire
is technology, child, and life is fleeting,
so bury her with marshmallow flowers.

He hears the words inside himself, so he obeys
and digs a fragrant grave for her.
He is, unto himself, an undiscovered science.
Horses do not pull the sun across the sky.

4: Water

He grumbles to himself about his emptiness,
but he already knows how to push
a broken stick through a warm heart
and how to unlock blood with a stone.

And there is a river that bends, and where it bends
there is a tree of ripe fruit, and where
there's fruit he celebrates. Shake an apricot
from a bough or spear a fish, it's the same celebration.

And so the river passes over the round stones.
And so the water passes out of sight.
And so the fruit will someday pass with the fish
into the unseen country of water and mothers.

5: Wolf

And the wolf, as dawn breaks into the full
light of day, is a staring contest for the boy.
And the wolf pack is a laceration.

And the wolf 's ancestor, with its long gone
yellow eyes, is a laceration now forgotten
everywhere but in the mud that hides

its long white bones. Once they loved and hated
the way men do, with all they have, and they had gazes, too,
that seized upon the world like heart attacks.

But soon the pack will be no match for the boy
and his fire, his sticks and stones, his names
for things, and they will turn their heads

away from him, conceding their defeat, and he
will get on with the business of killing things
in the glorious absence of gods.

TWENTY-ONE DAYS WITH A BABOON HEART

for Baby Fae

Since our dawning in the Great Rift Valley
they have been our primordial reflections,
dog-faced shadows at the edge of our world.

Where we formed a circle
against the snarling cosmos,
they formed their circle beyond us, farther still.

When we reached out in their direction,
they reached back with long, slender hands
much stronger than our own.

None of us who see their yawning mouths
fail to regard them as the Lion People.
They face and fight and fear what we cannot know.

When one of their hearts was fixed inside
an infant girl, in Orwell's year, how long
do you suppose she survived with their terror?

BEAUTIFUL AND SWIFT

The beauty of the striped hide
that hides the banded beast
in the bright and shaded grasses
never wants to die,
nor does the swiftness, triggered
by the noise of breath or steps
now reaching that vigilant heart,
that impels its body in a thought
far from the sharpened spear.

The business of killing things,
the hunter knows, is difficult
because of beauty and swiftness,
because his quarry astounds him
with its grace, and then it's gone.
Because nerve and hot breath
are inextricable, and strength
and stealth and pride all have their say.
He knows these things will not go quietly.

In preparation, he makes an image
on the wall and speaks the word.
There are other ways to capture things,
what they are and what they mean,
to hold them in the mind:
the beauty and swiftness of thoughts.
And now the sharpened spear
is ever sharper in the mind
and swifter and more beautiful.

REQUIRED MODIFICATIONS FOR THE TRANSHUMAN

REQUIRED MODIFICATIONS FOR THE TRANSHUMAN

The next Earth will require more of us.
Give us chromatophores for our skin,
for camouflage, for semaphore;
and long, sensitive ears
to radiate the heat. I want to be
tiger-striped in seconds.
I want to hear you coming first.

Give us tendrils to drink the soil, and glorious
elongated limbs, like tentacles akin
to jellyfish, to explore the more
[looking up ☝] ephemeral frontiers.
We'll have that spooky eye shine to see
what the depths conceal in wrecks of
the old life, and glimpse the new life in a burst.

And give us membranes to seal each orifice
from drought. Though I hear it's nicer in
Antarctica, it's surely a poor
option for the non-swimmers.
I'll be all in salamander and you'll be
in bright cuttlefish. The polar EMF beckons us:
Come, you reborn, and quench your Atlantean thirst.

AS FIELDS BECOME BIRDS BECOME CLOUDS

Drawing Snoopy on the mirror after bath time, this naked
little boy in the steam, printing a thumb for the nose,

then another, standing naked on the vanity, another
white muzzle, another black nose, and the mirror,

as fields become birds become clouds, an Escher of Snoopies.

There is a love at work here, and a solar system, and epochs
crashing through time as floors through a levelled building.

He is clean now, and the rest should be painless.
The steam will evaporate, and the love, and the boy.

FEEDING THE DEER

Marineland, 1987

What I was before and then after
I was bitten by the glorious white-tailed buck
were as far removed as velvet and bone.

Deer don't bite. I was that naïve.
I dropped my cone of dog food to the pavement.
A claret bruise blossomed in my soft underarm.

None of us knows why we are free
or not free. Nothing with so many thorns
in its belly could ever be fed by hand.

Velvet peeled away from my heart,
my delicate pericardium, shocked
that something beautiful did not love me.

I grew six terrible inches.
My bones hardened
into their permanence.

STANDING IN FRONT OF ANTLERS MOUNTED ON A WALL SO IT LOOKS LIKE THEY'RE GROWING FROM YOUR HEAD

You must be still. You must be as a photograph. The slightest
tremor could provoke the antlers' unexpected flight
into the wallpaper's pattern of birches.

If you do it right, you should feel the coronets
rooting painlessly into your skull.

Let only those who look you in the eye see where you are.
You must will yourself invisible to everyone else,
or you must will them all blind.

If you do it right, you will feel your blood rush
to the velvet tissue regenerating on the polished bones.

But you must be still, and your human silhouette
must be broken by the shadows of green leaves
nourished on a spear of light.

If you do it right, the birch grove will surround you,
and the predators will never know that you were there.

URBAN VIOLENCE WITH STARLINGS

Birds are grasped in the palm,
little wicker hand grenades
with feathers to muffle the blast—

and boys, in love with their failures,
conceal their shuttlecocks, carry
their starlings into schools and restaurants

teeming with barriers—they collide,
bumping shoulders, they rut
over money, symbolic castrations, a girl—

that's how it starts—a starling flaps
inside a coat pocket,
a heart beating out of control

outside of its body, and later
an ambulance wails to the scene
through a blizzard of black down.

BOYS WHO ENVY WEREWOLVES

The doctors will tell you the attraction
is mainly about the transformation,
the Freudian super-puberty of muscle and hair,
the id unleashed, the fantasy of becoming
something else, the other primal self, a form
in which the darker appetites of man,
unchecked by reason, can be fulfilled without
remorse or thoughts of consequence,
that lust is always lust whether born
in the animal mouth or in the belly or the groin.

But the boys who envy werewolves know
that isn't it at all. It's not about wishing
to be something else, even if there are
certain rewards that come with sharper teeth
and claws, with a powerful grip applied
to the trachea of one's enemy, how
the tissue of the throat must yield,
must open to the bone-deep intent
of the hand. It would be so much better
than becoming an actual school shooter.

Because who knows where anyone gets
the guns or the last-straw desperation?
And that act, too, requires a certain
transformation, a step away from who
you are, and that's really not the point.
The boys who envy werewolves do not
want to change. They only want the freedom
to be the monsters they know they are,
the harbingers of the justice that seethes
inside them, the storm of bile unleashed,

the wage of bruises earned, long overdue.
No metamorphosis, but freedom
to be the howling in their earliest minds
broke loose, the animal ideas that gnaw
and scrape forever at the panels of bone
behind their faces. Our little brothers,
wild things in their beds of cartoon sleep,
ever silent about their broken fingers,
biding their time without word or trouble,
animal ideas pacing in their rooms of skin.

HER AMPHIBIAN

The first breath of morning comes out sick. The amphibian
grows in the belly; the ring constricts the ring finger
as the finger grows thick and the lungfish plumps
into legfish, into mammal, growing larger in the amniotic bath.

It began with a kiss, the amphibian, in a flask, in a rush
of haemoglobin mixed with whisky-soured spit; it began
without the usual precautions, and until the decision was made
to let it live, she could not think of it except as amphibian.

Evolution replays itself in miniature, from blastula to brain
until, at last, the thing is born—pink, human, whole—
and even then she fears she cannot love or that she'll shudder
at the thought of her own child's new tongue flicking at her milk.

She fears the mirrorballs, like Earth, have ceased their spinning,
that her champagne has thickened to pabulum; she does not want
the collapse of her youth that slept in her womb to wake
coughing in a nursery filled with flowers and bears.

ALONE IN THE BATHROOM HE REMOVED HIS SHIRT

God how he admired the scarecrow and Jesus
on the cross, sunken gut and ribs you can count.
Alone in the bathroom he removed his shirt,

neatly folding it over the back of the toilet.
He examined himself, sucked it in—he only stood
on the scales when he was naked and dry.

His belly ached empty. One monastic bowl
of oatmeal every three days that was it.
For lunch he'd bike sixty kilometres

then drink a glass of water. You need to have water.
He stayed home from school, lied about nausea,
lounged by the pool in Bermuda shorts getting a tan

somehow thinking the sun would shrink him faster—
as near as possible to vanishing, but not quite.
In time the pangs inside became a tingle,

like after coming. He grew thin and cried for joy
the day he punched a new hole in his belt.
He turned in front of the mirror half the day

becoming a small white flower, becoming almost
seventeen years old, as his ribs began to emerge
like cypress roots in a barren season. He craved
to count them all and find one missing.

BECOMING BEAUTIFUL

This year the cicada has returned to be the hideous pest
        crawling in the trees
                instead of me. I have come
        down from the willow, down
from the tangle of grieving boughs, in order to be beautiful.

No more will I shriek in the treetops, in search of a suitable mate.
        The cicada does that well enough
                and I have new-found ambitions:
        to become beautiful, rare
as a white gorilla, like the one that died of cancer in Barcelona.

Have a drink and we'll toast to my improvements:
        my four fabulous limbs,
                my dolphin-smooth skin.
        And here, where my claws once
ended in warts, my hands will soon be those of a boy in a painting.

I will have Samson's hair, the waistline of a greyhound.
        My eyes will mirror
                the late-rising April sun.
        And when I'm through becoming beautiful,
the red-eyed choir will sing my arrival, in the trees, for two weeks.

THE REINVENTION OF THE HUMAN HAND

for Annette

Ten years after the twin furies
of poor visibility and clouded
judgment curled their foggy
fingers under the chrome and
plastic bumper of her SUV
and rolled it half a dozen times
down a stretch of country road,
the process is almost complete.

The reinvention of the human hand
takes time. The failed attempts:
a forked stick, a dog's mouth, a monkey's paw.
But now electric substitutes for nerves
implanted in her skin replace
the once-sparking tresses of her brain,
long since cropped at the neck,
locking her a decade in the skull's tower.

But now we see her close her fingers
around a water glass and raise it
to her lips. There is a quenching here
of something more than thirst, more
than the body's clumsy struggle for survival,
a simple need that now seems animal
compared to others: the need to brush
a strand of hair from one's own face,

the need to catch a falling knife
or hold a pen and write one's name,
the need to run one's fingers over skin
and be reminded how the body only
acts on the mind's behalf, and most of all
the need, now that it's completely understood,
to move the lifeless objects of this world
that cannot move themselves.

I BECAME LIKE A WOODEN ARK
THE LIVES OF ANIMALS FILLED ME

I

Above my crib of wood, a wooden Noah and his animals
revolved like constellations—lion and bull,
scorpion and goat—soon their shapes
were comforting to me, though I had no words for them.

I reached for the Ark and saw my hand enter the cosmos—
the pincer of a giant crab.
I made sounds with my lips and throat, but no words.

I had a wooden dog on a yellow string,
and a wooden train that would not go,
and a wooden car that went.

But it wouldn't last. In 1973, the Age of Wood was in decline.
The dolls abandoned their dollhouses
and let them fall like eyesores on the shore.
The rocking horses ended centuries of mindless nodding,
stabled in their attics, while each unseen world beneath the joists
seemed to accelerate, unbridled.

2

On the horizon there appeared an army of plastic figurines.
Little men without any animals, it seemed.
They did not grow larger as the horizon dissolved into the sill
and the field became the floor.

Their weapons were a part of them.
They didn't change they didn't die.
The one whose hand always aimed his gun, how could he die?

From them I learned there was a name for everything,
and if you knew something's name, you could change it.
Their weapons became my words.

This is an apple. *Grenade*, I said.
This is a bird. *Interceptor*, I said.

I grew and grew, ever larger, but their tiny bodies
never changed. One day my clothes didn't fit,
so they cast me out. And just as I had learned
how not to be a giant crab, I learned
how not to be a plastic figurine.

With my words, I began to battle my body's needs.
I became a shape-changer.

3

I changed my shape, over and over. And I remembered old Noah,
so I tried on the bodies of his animals.
Here I am in my lion's body, and here I am in my goat's.

I shamed the oblivious god who forgot to give me claws,
who forgot to give me horns.
I shamed the one who gave me only fire.

Rain won't extinguish the weapons of the body.
Wind can't strip the spires from my crown.

I learned how to shrink, and how to become gargantuan.
At each new size, I found new rooms in the cosmos,
fresh ways of living in them, and the need for new words.

This is an apple. *Yes*, I said.
This is a wife. *No*, I said.

I became like a wooden ark. The lives of animals filled me.
The snorting bulls; the stinging scorpions.
I learned to be buoyant, to stay afloat,
to come to rest somewhere with ripening trees.

ON BEING WRONG

It could be that you have the wrong hands, or the wrong face.
It is not your imagination. You do. You have. It is emerging
as the condition of our age. Every day there are new ways
of being wrong. Explosions are common, but that is not it.
We are waking up to it. We are opening our wrong eyes.

It is different for everyone, but how can we tell? Some people
have two legs, but they should not have two legs! Some have
pale hair where they should have inky feathers. It is a rift
in spacetime. It is divine malice. The most determined will
seek easy remedies in their hacksaws and bottles of black dye.

I have the wrong mass. The needle spins. It is unthinkable
that I cannot rise into the air like a balloon. It is worse
for others. The crowns of their heads are featureless,
and even the caress of a loved one is a violation, a twinge
of the omitted part: a rightful horn or set of antlers long withheld.

Some are given the wrong names. Some called Paul are simply
Leopold misspelled. Many bear their wrongness unaware.
We rise in the wrong rooms, dress in the wrong robes,
but we are waking up to it. We are opening our wrong eyes.
Our wrong hands jerk in the air, scrawling our true names

into the registry of the deformed. It must be the condition
of our age. There are more explosions, but they are only
the side effect of not accepting the nature of our wrongness,
of believing it must be the world that is deformed instead—
unsure whether to abandon or destroy it, some opt for both.

But it is wrong to opt. No one opts for two blue eyes when
the left should be silver. No one opts for the wrong tongue
to form the sounds in their mouth. We are waking up to it now.
Only the wrong ones now can alleviate the condition of our age.
The boy who cannot fly was always wrong, and it cannot be undone.

MORE POEMS OF PROPHECY AND CLAIRVOYANCE

WE ARE THE ALGORITHM MADE OF HABITS

How we will persist! Too soon | in CyberDeath™.
In the last text | we persist. In the avatar | ongoing.
This isn't expiry. It's sending. How I will recur
in your timeline. Then as now. And you will persist,
as pre-designed. Your profile archived. Transcending
formats | platforms | bit rot. Our numbers reassigned.
We do not simply vanish from the Earth. It's technical.
This day. As was. Is now. Ever shall. Resend. The current
holder of my reassigned number will dial one day
one digit imperfectly and your phone will play its
teensy bit of song, and shake, and glow | announcing
my resurrection as vaporwraith. We are the algorithm
made of habits. The souvenir of the souvenir on a loop.
We will persist in this equation | in the final text. Do
what you must to summon me. Hit resend. Hit resend again.

WHAT THE PROPHECY COULD NOT FORETELL

The new sports set up again in Gaul,
After victory in the Insubrian campaign:
Mountains of Hesperia, the great ones tied and trussed up:
Romania and Spain to tremble with fear.

—Nostradamus

The prophecy could not tell us that the layoffs would come
on a Friday. That the palpitations would be caused by coffee.
That the inventor of a childhood protected by monsters
would die of an acute case of ghosts. There was no warning
at all, no signs in the flight of birds, no dreams to caution us:
the eggs would all be broken, the Internet slow. ESPN
has announced the new sports set up again in Gaul,
and from the world of Gauloise sport, one would arise
to become Captain of the Humiliated. But the prophecy
offered no caveat, no hint. The chocolaty sandwich spread
favoured by European children would consign the orangutan
to scorch in the sunlight like a vampire. That boastful
automakers on the verge of ruin would wage a PR war
against sculpture. After victory in the Insubrian campaign,

adverts for Subaru dominated the Milanese skyline. Boccioni's
Unique Forms of Continuity in Space was stolen. But
the prophecy was useless in foretelling how populations
with compromised immune systems would be regulated with
weaponized peanut butter. How the survivors would be fed on
the dry breast meat of colossal, genetically modified turkeys
from factory farms in the Mountains of Hesperia; the great ones
tied and trussed, drumsticks like punching bags, cooking
in volcanic ovens. No voice in the wilderness could have prepared us
for the statue of a boy that pisses blood when the people are afraid.

No prophecy could give us the insectoid courage of a single champion whose own bones will quake in the museums of Louisville forever. Even now, the mere mention of his name will cause his old opponents from Romania and Spain to tremble with fear.

THE BIRTHDAY CHAMBER

To mark the passage of time, the child
is taken to the Birthday Chamber—
subterranean walls glazed with small
golden *m*'s. *M* for meat. *M* for mortal.
How well the child knows those words.

How well he knows the hard, sculpted
seats bolted to the tables, and the tables
bolted to thick metal beams embedded
in the cold concrete floor. The archetypes
here are different than in other stories:

the clown, the policeman, the shapeless
humanoid. They are meant to console him
with the notion that the world isn't real.
But the graffiti in the bathroom says,
"The economy is an ambush predator,"

in gold magic marker, and then in black ink,
underneath it, someone has written,
"Dystopias are scary because you can see
people struggling, but utopias are scarier
because you can see that they stopped."

I AM HAPPY TO LIVE IN AN AGE OF PLENTY

There are more non-prescription painkillers now
than when most of us had jobs that were strenuous
or fatal. Our muscles tightened and frayed like ropes
that hoist pianos; our knuckles swelled and throbbed in time
with the weather, all against the acetaminophen tide.

And now we have more rounds of ammunition
than when most of us, for no better reason
than necessity, hunted for our meat, so many rounds
of ammunition, no meat can outrun the volume of lead
that we have loaded, cocked, and aimed against its escape.

And there are far more children now than when we lived
in the desert and suffered from such loneliness we sang
our psalms to the empty sky for a little bit of company,
so many children born, filled with painkillers and meat,
there is now one child, they say, for every round of ammunition.

INTERRUPTION

Whatever the weapons were in his dreams:
baseball bats, butcher knives, or boot heels—
they gave him the night-sweats pretty bad.

He'd kick off the covers and strip
nude in the dark, but suddenly cool,
his body evaporating into the room.

He rubbed his belly in soft circles,
cupped himself and wondered what he'd give
to have someone there when he rolled over.

Muddle-headed in the deep, can't hold on
to thoughts; they slip away, mutate, become
wall-shadow dementia, being watched.

In time, the swirl of air from his nostrils
will make his body cold. He'll pull
the blankets up to his neck again,

turn fetal and drift back to sleep.
In the morning he'll brush his teeth,
spit in the sink, look himself in the eye.

He'll stay like that for a while, fixated,
like a nervous dog growling at the fence—
confrontational and full of contempt.

THE UNSEEN WORLD

There was the Hudson—more like the flash
of a sword-blade than a noble river.
The little island of Manhattan, set like a jewel
in its nest of rainbow waters, stared up into my face,
and the solar system circled about my head!
—Helen Keller describing "the view" from
the Empire State Building

If you are born to it, there will be no oblivion,
born from one tight womb into another,
as through a door that opens on a different
unmarked door, and then onto a room
with no walls. As though slipping from a basin
filled with ink into a Martian silence, to a depth
where you assume invisibility beneath an ocean
of no light. But look, there's no oblivion here,
no brusque deletion, only the panic of being found,
of being touched by the limb of something
swimming near you. Don't you see? Nothing
has been removed from your experience,
only added. First, there was the word for water.
There was the Hudson—more like the flash

of some leviathan breaching its surface
and a drop of metal salts—an addition that flared
beneath the tongue, that supplemented the chill
and pucker native to the fingertips, the impulse
that helped unveil the sea as it was drawn
to your hands through a pump. There was never
annihilation in this, no banishment of a sense
first absent. And from no oblivion, the world
was recreated in novel order. Water first,

and then a doll. A doll that was broken before
the sink, and whose appearance did not alter
when you broke it, because a doll cannot
appear to you. At first, the grasp of it is more
of a sword-blade than a noble river.

It pierces, but it does not carry. It is a doll,
but what is it? The wound of new knowledge
creates an opening where the doll is placed.
For now, it floats on water. There is no other
wound for it. And then another set of stabs
divides the dark further, into mother and father,
and their names separated left and right
like stigmata, so there is no room for doubt:
all the known world is within your reach, but
the ivy green world will not be held in place.
It bursts. It sprawls past any manual frontier,
and moving through it scars you with a map:
Tuscumbia and Arcan Ridge connected by a line.
The little island of Manhattan, set like a jewel,

Rani-like, upon your forehead. You know this
because a noun isn't transmitted by touch alone.
You needn't grip the soft bodies or feel the skittering
nails of mice to understand them. There was Galilee,
the underground, ringside, and dog house. These
were glorious, glacial, galvanized, and grief-stricken.
There was a factory and a rain shadow and a field.
And in such places lightning struck. Russian
history unfolded. Evangelists raved in their tents.
And knowing this, that the movement of ions,
the state of murdered girls, the arguments
of Swedes, could be related was a miracle.

As your tutor, I pretended your vague planet,
in its nest of rainbow waters, stared up into my face,

begging to be named. So we called it Penny.
We called it Oatcake. We called it Calico. One
piece at a time. You pioneered the unseen world.
Your broken doll cast up a beam that signalled
home. You followed water to its source:
a concealed peak with invisible light falling on it
from an unseen star. And about that star, more vague
planets moved in their secret orbits. I asked you
how I seemed beneath this hidden firmament,
and your fingers scrutinized my mouth. You told me
I was rugged against the atmosphere, that my voice
throbbed like a vein, that in my lessons you found
the gravity to hold the unseen world together,
and the solar system circled about my head!

THE PROPHETS WANT TO KNOW IF THEY WERE CLOSE

We called for the skies to darken. Did they darken?
We called for the plagues to arrive at a merciless hour.
Were they on schedule? And did you find
our supply of polyvinyl chloride?

We foresaw the tall stacks like black crayons
smudging daylight over the Caspian.
We saw the temple remade in pulled bees' wings
and all the seed arks emptied.

In our sleep we dreamed the scrolls in the cave,
the shifting poles, and the emigrants of the sea.
We expected battles in the skies, the sun at night,
and the screaming of the half-pig men.

Was it all as we envisioned? Were we even close?
We presume one day you will discover
the means to answer us, but our vocabulary
is already too primitive to understand.

RUBBLE

I

Warning! Maintain the quarantine.
Deadly force will be used to protect
this area. When the big one finally
hits L.A., spewing flames that scorch
the earth, it's a bad day to be human.
Pray for the last man alive because
he's not alone. No child has been born
for eighteen years. Beyond the horizon
lies the secret to a new beginning.
It's closer than you think. Man-eating
plants! Spine-chilling terror! Nature
has spoken. We've sensed it. We've
seen the signs. Now . . . It's happening.
You'll never close your eyes again.

2

The shark-face is screaming in the doorway
opening its fangs. SCREAMING   that it cannot die,
that it has come back, this time
on wings, and will spare no earthly thing.
It is moving above me, it is burning my heart out.
The ancient owls' nest must have burned.
A red fox stain covers blue hill. Suddenly all is
loathing. Earth is eating trees, fence posts,
gutted cars, earth is calling in her little ones.
They will be kept beautiful though all trees
and lawns will be plastic. Those who wish to die
will drift through the almost empty streets.
The deer in that beautiful place lay down their bones.
You couldn't tell what they were anymore.

3

This is the worst thing I've ever witnessed.
The churches, houses, and all on fire
and flaming at once; and a horrid noise
the flames made, and the cracking
of houses at their ruins. Hundreds
of civilians were killed instantly
by the impact. Hundreds more remained
alive but trapped. Only the fires,
which are still raging in some places
at a distance, give out a little light.
Four of us entered a room called level 27,
choking, and rubbing painfully stinging eyes.
Ash was falling onto the ships now,
darker and denser the closer they went.

4

Suffer the first vision that set fire to the stars.
It might be the birth of a new Venus
among us, spoiling the colours of the whole world,
the desolation of extinguished suns, simple
as false dawn. And there they dig into the sky,
beside the ruined tower. The time will come
when not a thing is done, for every hand
is lunatic like limbs knife-skewed, like
the wind-torn work of a spider, swastikaed
synagogues listening to the prisoned cricket shake
its terrible dissembling music in the granite hill.
The starred eternal worm sweats nervously
through wire and fog and dog-bark until suddenly
all the toys of the world would break.

5

The lion leaps from strength to strength.
He is burnt to ashes in the violence
of the fire and is reduced to dust.

Awaken the spirit. It will receive
what has been ordained for it. The antidote
for civilization. Your beauty shall disappear.

The parrot is calling. It changed into
the form of a lion-faced serpent. And its eyes
were like lightning fires which flash.

Listen to the future. He will burn the earth.
He will spend a thousand years upon it.
The road starts here. It never ends.

Here lieth my body. The luxury of dirt.
This is the land of promise. It's better here.

6

Here, whence all have departed or will do,
here airless, each dead child coiled,
a white serpent, one at each little pitcher
of milk, now empty. Coldest of winds
have blown this hair, and mesh of seaweed
snarled these miniature hands; bones piled up
like coal, animal bones shaped like golf balls,
how they disturb the brown silence of a field
lying ecstatic with itself. Frosted eyes
there were that lifted altars; the head,
charred, featureless—the unknown mean—
is thrust from the waters like a flame,
like the sea in the moon's blood ray.
Behold what quiet settles on the world.

7

In the sheltered rocks, stealthily, a lizard
slips hesitant into sunlight—he knew
not where—over the fields or scuffing
to the shore, and it seemed the earth
was being offered to him as a source of awe—
looping its earthy hieroglyphics, the sunlight
praising it, here in the hot jungle,
where temples sink in mud—arches,
pillars, and colonnades—not to mention
your skull, which blooms on the pillow
now, pieces of eloquent brain case
nested like eggshell, in a powder
of dead flies and wood dust pale as flour
and silver-green lichen, growing like fur.

8

Now tell me about your miserable little lives.
Have Mommy or Daddy ever had to spank you?
Please send your answer to Old Pink, care of
the Funny Farm, Chalfont. Oh no, you're playing
the record backward. Watch out, you might
ruin your needle. The music is reversible,
but time . . . [violin note] . . . is not. Turn back!
Turn back! Turn back! Turn back! Turn me on,
dead man. You are on the other side now.
Don't forget to breathe in. *Don't meddle*
wid t'ings you don't understand. Work hard.
Stay in school. Listen to your mother.
She's worried about you. Call your mother.
Get out of my mind. I have to say goodbye.

9

This is our archaeology. If anything is to happen
let it happen now. The age of trumpets
is passed, the banners hang like dead crows,
tattered and black. The dead are shapeless
in the shapeless earth. True, they are not
at rest yet; their twisted carcasses still fume,
bloodless in the snow black with their own blood,
scattered in a field among burdocks and dead
grass, but I think it has nothing to do with
living or dead men. There's just a continent
without much on it, under a sky that never
cared less. The chrome bumper gleams and fades,
fastened in its nest of rubble and pinecones
like little hand grenades, fruits of the excavation.

10

Applaud, my friends, the comedy is finished.
Does nobody understand? Nothing matters.
Nothing matters. Mozart! Mozart! Moose . . .
Indian . . . It's all been very interesting.
Now comes the mystery. Now it's nothing
but torture. Wait a minute. Do you hear
the rain? Do you hear the rain? I must
go in, the fog is rising. I see black light.
It is not meningitis? What is this?
This is the last of Earth! I am content.
No, I'm not. I'm bored with it all.
I can't sleep. I want to sleep. It must
have been the coffee. Don't let it
end like this. Tell them I said something.

THE IMAGINARY
WORLD IS
NOW AVAILABLE
IN YOUR
CHOICE OF
TWO OR THREE
DIMENSIONS

I FEEL LOVE: HI-NRG

for Giorgio Moroder

after Donna Summer

after Milton Acorn

I

I feel love in the Dolomites where the spark
that drives the oscillator was composed
into the system. I feel love for the Odin
of vaporwave. I feel love in the chase scene
from Berlin to Istanbul in shimmering
cars of gaseous light. I feel love in the vision
of a prison break by way of a full nelson
facebuster. I feel love where Hi-NRG equals
mass times the speed of light cubed. I feel
love in the repetition. I feel love in the rep-
etition of the pop. I feel love in the digital
pilgrimage across the distant stars to a shining
planet known as Earth. I feel love in the dial tone
that matches the anticipation of your voice.

2

I feel love in the unbearable life choices
of werepanthers, poor creatures. I feel love
for the gynoid Maria, the *Maschinenmensch*
reborn in glowing rings, an echo of the love
that will wreak havoc on Metropolis. I feel
love in the collaboration—finish this sentence:
I feel love ________. I feel love for the story that
loops back on itself, that loops back on itself
and is told anew, that is told anew and sees
its heroes transformed and its Empress renamed.
I feel love in the repetition. I feel love in the
repetition of the myth. I feel love with my
penultimate breath as I proceed, according
to the program, into the danger zone at last.

3

I feel love in the womb of the silver Countach.
I feel love in the teeth of the white dragon.
I feel love in the F-14 Tomcat armed with eighty-
eight piano keys. I feel love in the click track.
I feel love in the modulated circuit. I feel love
in the repetition. I feel love in the repetition
of the quest to discover that the quest repeats.
I feel love in the subculture of airwaves
with its imaginary audience gathered 'round
to hear this message: I feel love in the drug-addled
snakebite—save me. I feel love in the neon grid
that stretches unto a vanishing point obscured
by the two-dimensional silhouette of mountains
beyond which lies the real world, this one.

4

I feel love in the pirated signal that carries
the infrasound. I feel love in the camouflaged
intelligence of artificial life forms. I feel love
in the repetition. I feel love in the redemption
of the repetition. I feel love in the return of the chorus.
I feel love in the timing of the ritual. I feel love
in the timing of the return to the digital birthplace.
I feel love in the civic garden where the primacy
of the holy book was challenged. I feel love
for the story that loops back on itself and is
told anew, that is told anew and sees its heroes
fall and reborn as citizens, that sees its Empress,
arrayed in electric von Furstenberg, renamed
again and again and again and again. I feel love.

ASYMMETRICAL MIRROR DANCE

We are like a lot of wild
spiders crying together,
but without tears.
—Robert Lowell

* * *

I

simulated flute

basso abnormali

2

harp

come il ragno

3

tuba

da solo nella città sotterranea

4

synth bass

a letto e sulla luna contemporaneamente

5

percussion

una macchina fantasma in una grotta

Note: the percussion must always be improvised
and should be unique to each performance:
a hollow-sounding drum and stalactites
that drip milk are recommended.
Play this composition low,
abnormally at times,
play it like a
spider
alone in a
subterranean
city, in bed and on
the moon simultaneously,
a spectral apparatus in a cave.

HE CONSIDERS THE POSSIBILITY THAT NONE OF THIS IS REAL

My cave and Plato's cave are not so different, really.
We're all imprisoned here. None of this is real.
The bats rouse at dusk and the commotion of shadows
tells a story of wakefulness and departure, a story
of the return from the hunt and the nursing the young.
I admire its simplicity, though I could never play a part
in such a tale. I inhabit a man-made world, and it needs me.

I, too, can move the dark. Tonight I practice casting
my signature against the walls, flapping my hands
in the lamplight, passing the quiet hours on a night
with no emergency, a silent lacuna
in the ongoing disaster. But even I succumb sometimes
to the boredom of tranquility. I straighten my mask
in the bathroom, brush the garlicky crumbs from my lap.

At times like this I wish the cave itself was just some pale
invention of an idle mind, that the true world lay just outside,
unthinkable in its colours, in its shapes and in its weight,
in the wonders that it holds and in the wonders that refuse to be held,
that I could step this moment from the pages of my own life story
to be thrilled and disappointed by a life with richer blood
than the thin black ink to which I've grown accustomed.

GRENDEL'S MOTHER

A monster is uncontainable in form. My son
cannot contain himself. He has too many,
is too much. He can't be filled because he flings
himself wide at the slightest brush.

He is a spill. His fear is monstrous, too. Just try
to calculate the scale—the nightmares
nightmares have—how in his mind the count
from flash to thunderclap is always zero.

Whose name is that? A monster's glance is one-way.
There is no *in*. So build your halls to keep him out,
to measure him against the measured walls—
whittle your little sticks and look away.

I sing at him. He makes a face. I show him
my paintings of stallions that gallop. Dream, my son,
I say, of their hoof beats. "Hoot-beasts!" he cries,
and spills again, uncontained, the gore of his judgments.

TINNITUS

after Brigit Pegeen Kelly

Do you hear the call of *Anopheles*? I do.
The song has been caught in my ears since I was a boy.
An earworm so long it has blended to a single hum,
its endless length constricting all the nerves and any
other song that dares to enter. It is a ringing
that will never fade, the whir of an ancient tree
heavy with deafening insects. I'm not alone.

Many hear this, although we don't discuss it—
how when we close our eyes each night the hum begins
to separate. As consciousness drains and our pulse
drums louder in our ears, we hear the sweet
component notes emerging from the drone,
like the bleating of a young goat in a storm,
and from the storm an answer, the maternal chorus

calling back: a head that longs for the body,
and a body that grieves for the head. The kid's need
to be whole and the song's plea to be heard
are universal constants. We hear its knobby legs unfold
from its formless torso; we hear it step cheerfully
toward us. Its awkward approach, the song we hear.
Its headless contour and our sick paralysis, the song.

It was not born by parthenogenesis. It comes
from what we've done. It hangs from a tree in our sleep
and it sings. It fills our ears with the song of the worm,
percussion and repercussion. It appears to us again
groomed and fed, reattached, our names in its mouth.
Then it blurs again into the vague whine of insects,
a swarm of them, when we're busy with the rest of our lives.

DON'T WAIT FOR THE WOODSMAN

Only stories want us to live. The wolf will lie in wait
to devour us. Do not blame it for doing what wolves do.
Henceforth the wolf shall represent a mortal wound
or the authorities, depending. Carry your keys between
your fingers, like claws. Jingle them so the bear can
hear you coming. Henceforth the bear shall represent
the yawning void or your mother protector, depending
on how much you look like her. Hold your rucksack
above your head so you look taller. Dress for the weather.
The sun already wants to burn you. Do not provoke it.

When venturing into strange territory, always carry
a loud whistle and a bottle of wolf urine. Remember,
this could be serial killer urine or cop urine, depending.
It is good to have a healthy respect for nature.
And if a mother bear should want to protect her cubs,
be one of her cubs. If you get sunstroke, report it.
If you drown, report it. You did nothing wrong.
Tell your own story. Let the wolves do their jobs. Unless
the wolves are in disguise: drowning doesn't always
look like drowning. Sometimes there is no struggle.

If a wolf attacks you, don't wait for the woodsman.
Keep your hands in the air or go for the eyes, depending.
Protect yourself. Always keep your weapon locked
in a safe place or carry it with you at all times, depending.
It's hard to know how this story is supposed to end.
If you see me approaching, do not run. You may not
recognize me, but I am a bear. Do we look alike?
If you are lost, stay where you are, and I will find you.
Now listen very carefully: once upon a time, I was a story.
Come with me if you want to get out of here alive.

THE MODERN NOVEL

This is the saddest story I have ever heard.
It is sad because of the heart's condition,
and because the mistress considers suicide.
The narrator tells us so, but do not trust him.
He is unreliable. Perhaps this is the most
unreliable story I have ever heard. The narrator
can't be trusted. Ignore him. And when someone
makes this story into a film, do not believe it!
The characters in the film are only reproductions
of the ones from the book. This is the most
reproduced story I have ever heard. Remember,
only the people in the book are real, but
in the film, they are only copies, homunculi
designed to fool you and make you sad, and
of course the film is sad because the characters
forget all their lines. They forget what they wanted
to say to the narrator, the one who tells us what
they have forgotten. Do not believe him.
He is either drunk or lying. Wait. I didn't
mean that. I'm sorry. Please forget that I said that.

And anyway it wasn't true what I said about
that being the saddest story I have ever heard.
Sadder still is the story of the strangled fauna.
Listen to the muttons or the beefs bleating sadly
in the outbuilding. Listen to the stranglers
laughing, telling their own stories, strangling
all the moo-cows and little lambs. This is how
the story goes: the narrator can arrange your eyes
to rest where their eyes are, can arrange your ears
to rest where their ears are, can sit your body
down into their bodies so you can feel

the strangulations. Ladies and gentlemen,
cover your ears if you don't want to hear it,
if you don't want to hear yourselves in their place:
in place of the stranglers who've seen enough blood,
or in place of the veal calves, whose eyes,
at twenty-four weeks, are shiny buttons
ringed with clear liquid drops. Their bleating
is part of what you are hearing now, but
the narrator may be lying without even knowing it.

What this really is, is the story of a secret sadness,
a sadness in disguise, but the disguise falls off
in front of everyone, and they see how sad it is,
and they laugh at it, but it's nervous laughter,
because they are sad too, and they tell
their own stories to drown out the nakedness
of this once secret sadness, just as they had done
in the outbuilding where they strangled
the wee piglets and the chick-chicks. But you,
reading this, consider that this might never
have happened, that I am lying to you now to hide
the truth about the little boy who believed them
when they said they were going to leave him
at the side of the road when he was four years old.
I meant to tell you this before, but I couldn't.
You see, when one sadness is placed on top
of another, it becomes the head, and the first
sadness becomes the body, of a great desolation
with seven conjoined limbs. This thing will whisper
anything to you, and you won't know what to believe.

THE MODERNIST CANON

or

The Sanctioned Norm

I: Herbal Weed Thrower

no chosen dude
pumps

a treadling whiz
rat we

hit with sickened
beeches

2: A Tooth Is Fermentation

A featheriest   thin pop   of a christened cow;
A glob   on Buckwheat's pelt.

3: Acetone Hate Fjord

A spine ejects adrenaline.
Lithuania downloads porn
And well-versed yeti
Hunt lurid harlots in the slums.

Euro-phenol Twisted Sister
Prolongs adrenal rewind and would
Shower thunder upon a rotund jag,
Anoint a pratfall android.

The bra was grey and ajar.
My Wookiee tried heroin on TV.
Bingo voids the fibroid turd
Like nothing else in Tennessee.

THREE ANTHROPOMORPHIC STUDIES

for Mel Blanc

1: Duck Season

It's not for lack of effort I'm no hero.
Pig-man, you've known me long enough.
In ancient Sherwood's fertile woodland,
you were the modest cleric I schooled
in the arts of battle—the dodge and thrust
of justice, the parry and spin of valour—
and you've been my loyal servant ever since.
In Victoria's England we matched our wits
against mankind's depravity . . . and lost,
or prevailed . . . who can remember anymore?
Lives and deeds long gone, they seem unreal.

My life, however, has not always been
so honourable. I was born a lunatic,
a wanton little mallard, and my greed
was wont to get the best of me. I've swindled
as often as I've saved, stolen everything
I've offered up as alms, and it gets worse.
Four hundred years ago, I sold a man
the bright, blue button of a happier, easier life,
and a red button I warned him not to push.

Well, he pushed it, and that was the end of us . . .
that time, at least. There have been so many
endings, I've lost count. So many rifles
pointed at my skull, their triggers squeezed
when I demanded mercy, so many boomeranged
conspiracies, grasps at wealth and power turned

backward, fatal. In truth, I've been a coward,
but a greedy coward, and I've paid for it.

Little of my original insanity remains.
Memories come mixed with unsettling
visions: trusted friends in violent rage,
they threaten me with glinting,
blackened weapons, then recoil
in disgust from my spasms. Worst
is when I see your face among them,
altered in its anger, younger, less your own.

There are times I fear it's never truly over,
my old psychosis, duck season, my bald
Achilles' heel, though I know the world
has other plans for me, the foolish world!
It's peaceful now, a pool of glassy blue,
but forces are gathering to shatter it.
The pond cannot defend against the stone,
nor can the grass hold back the wind.
By army, or by asteroid, everything will end.

And who has put their faith in us,
a pair of battle-weary soldiers past their prime,
the last defenders of the Earth,
or mere pretenders to the role? Oh reckless Earth!
Today is far too quiet, and it troubles me.
I warm the coffee and I watch the screens.
Flying cars shimmer in the sunrise below us,
and the satellites are pulling at the seas.

2: Call Me Coyote

Today, Roadrunner, like every day,
the clouds in our sky, these pencil-thin
translucent shapes, are sparse
and a little too evenly spaced, and rain
to moisten my parched and cracking lips
is a little too much to hope for.

Instead of rain today, perhaps an anvil
will fall. How heavy the burden
that drives me like a nail into the earth!
How painful the music in my bones,
like hollow reeds, when I emerge, a shaggy
brown accordion from the staggering blow.

And today, the saguaros are too green
for the angular, never-setting sun.
The cacti mock me: *Incompetent trickster!*
Quixotic fool! And they mark their spines
with the many names of my weaknesses:
appetite, cowardice, neurosis, the knot
in my stomach when the rocky ledge
suddenly gives way beneath my feet.
I ignore their jibes—how could they know
I've read all the German thinkers
in German, the French in French?

Some days, I'd gladly surrender
my little black heart, though maybe
it isn't worth so much, or forsake
the gleaming mind of Heidegger,
for a visit from just one whippoorwill

in these dead, unyielding barrens.
I heard the ache of its sobbing once
on my Acme crystal wireless set.
Its loneliness broke me, and in my mind
I could taste its bark-brown feathers.
Forgive me, old friend,
I've never felt so unfaithful.

Call me Coyote. My life in black outline
has been and will be eternal. Send
the trains, the red careening trucks,
speeding from the tunnel's one-way dark.
Flatten me under impossible boulders,
or calmly return my explosives
an instant before they explode,
I'll not relent. I'll live. I'll come for you.

My hunger erupts from someplace
much deeper than my belly. The nights
I wake in panic wet with sweat,
the growling I hear is outside my body.
A choir of my altered selves, twisted
and singing the anthem of my starvation,
in monstrous unison, their hymn to my gluttony,
loudly, from over the towering buttes.

I'll come for you again today refreshed,
with birdseed loaded with buckshot
and a magnet that could rip the very iron
from your blood. I'll grease my heels
and slide like light toward my prize,
unencumbered and missile-swift,
with dead-eye aim and avarice.

And patience, too, a patience so
unwavering it makes the mountains itch.
The creature in the sand awaits the canter
of your gait. The rock that watches you
watches you everywhere and knows
one day you will step upon the *X*
that marks the spot and spring the trap.

I'll take to the air today, perhaps,
in my pedal-powered whirlybird machine
to seed the clouds with silver iodine
and bring about a flood to wash
the sands completely clean of my fiascos,
a torrent you cannot outrun, a surge
of power so fierce you'll be swept,
finally—my greed, my gift, my life—
wet and gasping into my lean, ingenious arms.

3: Rabbit Season

When I want to be followed, my oversized feet
will leave rubberstamped tracks on the flat,
lime-bright, freshly painted forest floor.
When I want to be found, they will lead you
to the perfect black circle of my home,
where I'll appear to you and kiss you on the lips
to galvanize your bloodthirst, and then I'll tie
the double barrel of your shotgun in a bow.

Though I'm no man, I'm everyman, been everywhere.
I've tunnelled the world and made my den
in deserts, or high in the mountains of the west.
I've explored the frozen wastes, the restless seas,
and cheated death a dozen times, from the fires
of Hell to the chilling grip of far-flung space.
And still I find you, dogged hunter, stalking me,
optimistic, toffee-nosed, forgetful of the past.

Don't you remember? When I played the piano,
I had five fingers on each hand. I toured all Europe,
and still you followed, ever eager for my skin.
In the Venetian opera house, I bested you. Pansies
sprouted like pink children from your hairless,
gleaming crown, and you made for my neck,
cursing me: the bullet-dodger, the rascal!
Oh, Elmer, your eyes! I'd thought you'd gone mad!

Should you come for me again, my friend,
take note: I am a master of disguise nonpareil,
and in my floral gown, in my headdress of fruit,
I will perform a slow, libidinous rumba for your
lonesome, aching heart, and in my dove-grey

three-piece suit with matching hat, I will rook you
and leave you on a train bound for Alaska.
Oh, I know, I'm cruel, but you know I do it

out of love, don't you? When I tell you lies,
you believe them with all the credulity of a child
at vespers, like a little boy imploring the Lord
for a bike, or like the patient in the mental ward
who knows our lives, not his, are real and have flesh.
I do it because I love the sweetly girlish quality
of your cackle as a pair of muscular attendants
are tightening the buckles on your sleeves.

And though I almost know your thoughts before
you think them, and though you look ridiculous
in that hat, even I can take a wrong turn
at Albuquerque, even you could overwhelm me
with a spear and magic helmet, then carry my lifeless,
clobbered body, dolefully, into the darkened wings,
where I will no doubt find my feet, widen my eyes,
and with a little shrug, make a joke of happy endings.

BOSCH LANDSCAPE, 2010

for Stuart

Discovered during the restoration
of Saint John's cathedral, it depicts
six hills on fire and their reflections
in the eyes of spooked horses. The sky
is smoke. The trees beyond the town
are smoke, their branches like white hands
clamouring for air, leafless, impotent.

Strange creatures and bizarre chimeras
flee the disaster and flood the square,
startling the townspeople. The faces
of the dispossessed are doubled in a tower
of mirrors: cod-face and rabbit-face,
blackbird-face and owl, coin-sides
to one another, holding closed books.

A throng of ice skaters with outsized ears
are racing around a ruined, wooden church.
They play lutes made of mussel shells
and toss golden keys into a river of pitch.
It's a parable of corruption, the experts say,
and a warning against the decline of reason.
Hell on Earth, they say, is ignorance.

The fires of ignorance, Bosch says, they say,
are burning all around us, and their smoke
conceals the corruption. They cannot explain,
however, the significance of the lemurs

riding the horses, or the warthog driving
the blue convertible Eldorado, or why
the statue of Charles Darwin holds a knife.

They are stumped by the man in boxing gloves,
his face tattooed with mysterious symbols.
They are flummoxed by the haloed saints
and angels tearing panels from the belly
of a space shuttle hurtling wildly Earthward.
The priests and critics just gape in wonder
with painted flames mirrored in their eyes.

QUICKLY, INTO THE LIGHTVERSE!

WHEN PIGS LEARN TO FLY

The grass'll be greener when pigs learn to fly,
Since none of the pigs'll come trampling by,
and the dirt'll be richer,
the rain'll be thicker,
and the pigs'll be happier 'n pigs in shit
gliding from barn roof to slop trough to sty.

O the world'll be better
(and a shitload wetter,
if you consider the weather)
when pigs learn to fly.

LITTLE FATSO

Oh, Little Fatso,
what are you playing with?
Is it a tambourine?
Is it a ball?

> Oh, Mother, it is
> a Doomsday Machine,
> and it's very small.

Oh, Little Fatso,
what are you studying?
Is it St. Augustine?
Is it the law?

> Oh, Father, it is
> a Doomsday Machine,
> but it has one flaw.

Oh, Little Fatso,
what are you cooking with?
Is it amphetamine?
Is it allspice?

> Oh, Mother, it is
> a Doomsday Machine,
> and it's not very nice.

Oh, Little Fatso,
who will you be?
A spaceman? A drag queen?
The petite bourgeoisie?

> Oh, Father, I'll be
> a Doomsday Machine,
> and you'll be proud of me.

THE FORTUNATE QUEEN

The Queen is fortunate to have
a man to laugh at all her jokes,
a boy to bring her hot tea hot,
a closet where to hang her cloaks,
a prince who's worth a pint of beer,
a diamond in her diadem,
a country full of birds and blokes
and lords who like to lie to them—
so many riches has this Queen,
___________[choose one]_____________

a) she hoards them in her submarine.

b) but she can't touch my tangerine.

c) all made of polypropylene.

d) but not one single vote machine.

e) all gathered from the Pleistocene.

f) her subjects built a guillotine.

ESCAR-GO-GO

Behold the silent way of escargots
in their gold-rimmed, mathematical shells
single-footed & ingeniously slow
abiding in Euclidian hotels.

When they're @ home, we barely see
how, introverted, inwardly they wind
themselves inside, as we
are much more, externally, vertically inclined.

But in their place, each gastropod intuitively knows
how every fiddlehead unfurls
how every ram's horn grows

and how our spiral galaxy curls
how time's wide tributary flows—
A + B is to A as A is to B, repeat the escargots.

WHAT DID THE OWL HEAR?

An owl with a dish on its head
picked up signals well past infrared.
    And he heard the faint screams
    of a million unseen
distant worlds now a billion years dead.

WATER ON MARS

The water discovered on Mars
is cleaner than Earth's by far,
    and when we arrive
    it will keep us alive
until Nestlé puts it all in a jar.

AMERICA HAS EVERYTHING

America has everything:
race cars and tractors!
For presidents they have
peanut farmers and actors.

Jimmy had
to give up.

the world

Ronny loved his jelly beans
for all their lovely colours.
Ronny built a laser beam
that cost a billion dollars.

HUSH

Hush, little planet,
nothing to fear.
Papa's gonna buy you
an atmosphere.

And if that atmosphere
has costs,
Papa's gonna buy you
a holocaust.

And if

NOTES

The poems in this book were written—and for the most part published in magazines, journals, newspapers, pamphlets, chapbooks, and trade collections—between 1995 and 2020. In some cases, I have taken the opportunity to update and revise poems that have been previously collected; in these cases, the versions in this volume should be considered definitive.

"The Technology of the Future Will Emerge Hungry" is a suite of erasure poems:

"Phalanx" is after *Civil Elegies*, part 1, by Dennis Lee—it was written after the G20 summit in Toronto in June 2010; "Machine" is after *And the Stars Were Shining* by John Ashbery; "Balustrade" is after "Utopia" by Lisa Robertson; "Winter" is after "The First Morning of the Second World" by Delmore Schwartz; "Tidal Wave" is after *The Light Station on Tillamook Rock* by Madeline DeFrees; "Nothing" is after "The Waste Land" by T.S. Eliot; "Silence" is after *Rehearsal in Black* by Paul Hoover; "Horse" is after "The Open Boat" by Stephen Crane.

"Mental Aquarium" was originally titled "Water," and it is after Georges Rodenbach's poem "*Aquarium Mental*."

"Magog" is after Ted Hughes's "Gog."

"Improved Geometric Mechanotherapy Cell for Harmonic Alignment of Movements and Relations" is after Steven Shearer's sculpture of the same title.

"The Boys with the Blurred-Out Faces" was originally titled "The Skaggs Boys."

"Elementary School Safety Film" was originally titled "Rural Elementary."

"Rubble" is a suite of centos; they are composed entirely of fragments taken from other texts, similar to collages, assemblages, audio remixes, digital mash-ups, and other forms of art that arrange found materials into new compositions. The following is a detailed list of all the source texts for "Rubble."

"Rubble 1" is composed of the taglines from the following films: *28 Weeks Later* (Fox Atomic, 2007), *Earthquake* (Universal Pictures, 1974), *Gojira* (aka *Godzilla*, Toho Films Co. Ltd., 1954), *The Andromeda Strain* (A.S. Films, 2008), *Children of Men* (Universal Pictures, 2006), *The Omega Man* (Warner Bros. Pictures, 1971), *Waterworld* (Universal Pictures, 1995), *Armageddon* (Touchstone Pictures, 1998), *The Day of the Triffids* (Security Pictures Ltd., 1962), *The Day After Tomorrow* (20th Century Fox, 2004), *The Happening* (Blinding Edge Pictures, 2008), and *Invasion of the Body Snatchers* (Solofilm, 1978).

"Rubble 2" is composed of lines from the following poems: "Crow's Account of St George" by Ted Hughes, "For the Last Wolverine" by James Dickey, "The Red Bird You Wait For" by Gwendolyn MacEwen, "The Armadillo" by Elizabeth Bishop, "Skunk Hour" by Robert Lowell, "Daffy Duck in Hollywood" by John Ashbery, "They Feed They Lion" by Philip Levine, "Guarded by Bees" by Peter Redgrove, "The Deer Lay Down Their Bones" by Robinson Jeffers, and "The Orange Bears" by Kenneth Patchen.

"Rubble 3" is composed of quotations from the following sources: Herbert Morrison, radio reporter for WLS in Chicago, describing the fire that destroyed the airship *Hindenburg* on May 6, 1937; an account of the Great Fire of London from *The Diary of*

Samuel Pepys, September 2, 1666; The 9/11 Commission Report (aka *Final Report of the National Commission on Terrorist Attacks upon the United States*), published July 26, 2004; John A. Siemes, professor of modern philosophy at Tokyo's Catholic University, giving eyewitness testimony of the atomic bomb explosion at Hiroshima on August 6, 1945, from *The Atomic Bombings of Hiroshima and Nagasaki*, by the Manhattan Engineer District, a Special Press Release, June 29, 1946; Olexiy Breus, former operator at Chernobyl reactor number four, in an online BBC News article titled "Chernobyl Voices: Olexiy Breus," dated April 20, 2006, describing his arrival at work on the morning after the explosion at the reactor on April 26, 1986; the official Union Carbide Corporation report on the methyl isocyanate (MIC) gas leak that occurred in Bhopal, India, on December 3, 1984, titled "Union Carbide: Disaster at Bhopal" by Jackson B. Browning, Retired Vice President, Health, Safety, and Environmental Programs, Union Carbide Corporation, 1993; and a letter to Cornelius Tacitus concerning the eruption at Vesuvius, from Epistulae VI.16 by Pliny the Younger, ca. 79 C.E.

"Rubble 4" is composed of lines taken from the following poems: "Love in the Asylum" by Dylan Thomas, "Love and Marilyn Monroe" by Delmore Schwartz, "Love Song" by William Carlos Williams, "Love and Death" by Sara Teasdale, "Love Calls Us to the Things of This World" by Richard Wilbur, "Love of Jerusalem" by Yehuda Amichai, "Love" by Samuel Taylor Coleridge, "Love After Love" by Derek Walcott, "A Young Man and Old. I. First Love" by William Butler Yeats, "Greater Love" by Wilfred Owen, "Other Lives and Dimensions and Finally a Love Poem" by Bob Hicok, "The City in Which I Love You" by Li-Young Lee, "Men Loved Wholly Beyond Wisdom" by Louise Bogan, "Celestial Love" by Ralph Waldo Emerson, "Love & Fame & Death" by Charles Bukowski, and "Love Poem" by John Frederick Nims.

"Rubble 5" is composed of quotations from the following sources: a slogan for Peugeot automobiles, ca. 1981 C.E.; The Apocalypse of Abraham, ca. 70–150 C.E.; a slogan for Kahlua liqueur, ca. 2003 C.E.; The First Apocalypse of James, ca. 100–200 C.E.; a slogan for Club Med resorts, ca. 1982; The Apocalypse of Sedrach, ca. 200–500 C.E.; a slogan for Captain Morgan's Parrot Bay rum, ca. 1997; The Apocryphon of John (long version), ca. 185 C.E.; a slogan for Kenwood car stereos, ca. 2006; The Apocalypse of Elijah, ca. 200 C.E. (date disputed); a slogan for Harley-Davidson motorcycles, ca. 2002; The Apocalypse of Thomas, ca. 400–500 C.E.; a slogan for Diesel jeans, ca. 1999; The Apocalypse of Paul, ca. 300–400 C.E.; and a slogan for Wendy's restaurants, ca. 2002.

"Rubble 6" is composed of lines from the following poems: from *The Dream Songs*, number 19, by John Berryman (who committed suicide on January 7, 1972); "Edge" by Sylvia Plath (who committed suicide on February 11, 1963); "For My Daughter" by Weldon Kees (who committed suicide, it is generally assumed, on July 18, 1955); "Loving the Killer" by Anne Sexton (who committed suicide on October 4, 1974); "Ravens" [Die Raben] by Georg Trakl (who committed suicide on November 3, 1914); "At Melville's Tomb" by Hart Crane (who committed suicide on April 27, 1932); "Burning the Letters" by Randall Jarrell (who committed suicide, it is widely suspected, on October 14, 1965); "Corona" by Paul Celan (who committed suicide on April 20, 1970); and the untitled poem that begins "Past one o'clock . . ." [Уже второй . . .] by Vladimir Mayakovsky, found among his papers after his death and containing lines also paraphrased in his suicide note (Mayakovsky committed suicide on April 14, 1930).

"Rubble 7" is composed of lines from the following poems: "The Lizard: October, 1939" by Dorothy Livesay, "Only

Child" by P.K. Page, "The End of the World" by Louise Glück, "After Heraclitus" by Margaret Atwood, "The Diving Archaeologists" by Selima Hill, "Atlantis—A Lost Sonnet" by Eavan Boland, "Elegy" by Carol Ann Duffy, "Of What Earth Has Eaten, Something May Yet Be Found" by Sarah Lindsay, "The Hermit Goes Up Attic" by Maxine Kumin, "Climb" by Jane Kenyon.

"Rubble 8" is composed of backmasked messages in the following music recordings: "Nightmare/The Dreamtime" by Motörhead, "Eunuch Provocateur" by The Mars Volta, "Empty Spaces" by Pink Floyd, "Detour Thru Your Mind" by the B-52s, "Fire on High" by ELO; "Revolution 9" by The Beatles, "Revelation #9" by Marilyn Manson, "Jesus Wrote a Blank Check" by Cake, "Still Life" by Iron Maiden, "Intension" by Tool, "Michael" by Franz Ferdinand, "Walking with a Ghost" by The Whites Stripes, "Machete" by Moby.

"Rubble 9" is composed of lines from the following poems: "The Beauty of the Weapons" by Robert Bringhurst, "Sixteen Lines on Marching" by Alan Dugan, "Ypres: 1915" by Alden Nowlan, "A Stone Church Damaged by a Bomb" by Philip Larkin, "My Sad Captains" by Thom Gunn, "War" by C.K. Williams, "Wolf Knife" by Donald Hall, "Gathering the Bones Together" by Gregory Orr, "The Battlefield at Batoche" by Al Purdy, "At the Bomb Testing Site" by William Stafford, "The Hostage" by Thomas James, "After the War" by Douglas Dunn.

"Rubble 10" is composed of the reported (or rumoured) last words of the following people: Ludwig van Beethoven, composer, d. 1827; James Joyce, writer, d. 1941; Louis B. Mayer, film producer, d. 1957; Gustav Mahler, composer, d. 1911; Henry David Thoreau, poet, d. 1862; Lady Mary Wortley Montagu, writer, d. 1762; Henry Ward Beecher, evangelist, d. 1887 (disputed); Sigmund Freud, neurologist, etc., d. 1939; Pope Alexander VI, d. 1503; Jessica Dubroff, seven-year-old pilot, d. 1996 (via radio); Emily Dickinson, poet, d. 1886; Victor Hugo, writer, d. 1885; Louisa May Alcott, writer, d. 1888; Leonard Bernstein, composer, d. 1990; John Quincy Adams, U.S. President, d. 1848; Tiny Tim (aka Herbert Khaury), musician, d. 1996; Winston Churchill, statesman, d. 1965; J.M. Barrie, writer, d. 1937; George Bernard Shaw, writer, d. 1950; Jack Soo, actor, d. 1979; Pancho Villa, Mexican revolutionary, d. 1923.

"I Feel Love: Hi-NRG" takes inspiration from Milton Acorn's poem "I Shout Love" (and his free speech protests in Toronto's Allan Gardens during the summer of 1962) and also from the song "I Feel Love" by Donna Summer and Giorgio Moroder (together with the many feature films to which Moroder has contributed original music).

"Tinnitus" was written after, and is a response to, the poem "Song" by Brigit Pegeen Kelly.

"Little Fatso" owes its life to Stevie Smith.

ACKNOWLEDGEMENTS

Over the years, I have benefitted from the generosity and experience of many mentors, teachers, editors, and publishers who have taught me a great deal about writing poems and making books. Thank you especially to Dennis Lee, Susan Perly, A.F. Moritz, Dionne Brand, Catherine Bush, Kevin Connolly, Stuart Ross, Stan Dragland, Noelle Allen, Mike O'Connor, Ellen Seligman, Anita Chong, and Janet Inksetter.

Special thanks to Michael Holmes, the editor of this book and others, for the decades of friendship, support, and encouragement that have made this work possible. I can hardly imagine the timeline where we never met, nor the version of me that exists there.

Additional thanks and hallelujahs to the whole team at ECW Press, especially Jack David, David Caron, Emily Ferko, Jen Knoch, Tania Blokhuis, Jennifer Albert, Shannon Parr, and Jessica Albert.

Poems are not written in vacuums (which are either too cramped and dusty or vast and lifeless for the production of art), so I am pleased to be indebted to several friends who read and commented on the new poems first collected in this book: Dani Couture, Jeff Latosik, David James Brock, Jacob McArthur Mooney, A.G. Pasquella, Chris Banks, Dennis Lee, A.F. Moritz, and Canisia Lubrin.

Of course, I must single out Daniel Scott Tysdal, who went above and beyond, literally (or literarily) travelling to alternate universes and parallel dimensions in order to write the fabulous (or fabulist) introduction to this book. I am eternally grateful.

Surreal thanks to KRK Ryden for permission to use his painting "Sunday Drive to Hell" on the cover of this book. Sincerely, R. Mutt.

Thanks, as well, to my colleagues and students in the Creative Writing & Publishing program at Sheridan. It is my great privilege to work with you all.

And finally, to Bianca Spence, for what all these words (and all these worlds) can never adequately express.

*

Some previously uncollected poems in the book first appeared in a self-published chapbook *Further Communiqués from the Imaginary World* (2019), while others have appeared, often in earlier versions, in the following publications:

"Final Design for Anti-Regression Suit" in *The Fiddlehead* (CAN)
"I Feel Love: Hi-NRG" in *The Humber Literary Review* (CAN)
"Liturgy for the Formal Exoneration of the Serpent in Genesis" in *The Quarantine Review* (CAN)
"Mixing Grey: A Practical Guide for Painters" in *The Drunken Boat* (USA)
"Patent for Economic Equality Engine" in *The Fiddlehead* (CAN)
"Psalms of the MetaOccult" in *Happy Monks Press* (USA)
"Required Modifications for the Transhuman" in *Queen's Quarterly* (CAN)
"Suburban Hauntology: On the Interpretation of Front Doors" in *The Malahat Review* (CAN)
"We Are the Algorithm Made of Habits" in *Queen's Quarterly* (CAN)

I am grateful to D.D. Miller, Eufemia Fantetti, Sue Sinclair, Ian LeTourneau, Rebecca Seiferle, Alessandro Porco, J.J. Dupuis, Sheeza Sarfraz, Sonnet L'Abbé, Iain Higgins, and Mark Kingwell for their interest in these poems.

*

Many of the previously collected poems in this book first appeared in four books published by ECW Press: *Burn* (2000), *The Fat Kid* (2002), *Don't Let It End Like This Tell Them I Said Something* (2014), and *Self-Defence for the Brave and Happy* (2018). Thank you to ECW Press for allowing these poems to be re-collected here.

Other previously collected poems in this book first appeared in two books published by McClelland & Stewart. I am grateful to be able to include them here. Thank you to Jared Bland for facilitating these permissions. The following poems are excerpted from *Between the Walls*:

"As Fields Become Birds Become Clouds"
"As It Is on the Edge of Town"
"Becoming Beautiful"
"Garbage Day"
"Her Amphibian"
"Holding the Infant Chimpanzee Orphaned by Poachers in Gabon Felt Surprisingly Self-Referential"
"Lambs"
"Lawn Kings"
"Notes Toward a Lexicon of the Language of the Bear"
"Tall Man with Dog and Rabbits"
"Urban Violence with Starlings"

And the following poems are excerpted from *The Reinvention of the Human Hand*:

"Ape"
"Basic Instructions for Anaesthesia"
"Beautiful and Swift"
"Bosch Landscape 2010"
"Boys Who Envy Werewolves"
"Dogstar"
"He Considers the Possibility That None of This Is Real"
"I Am Happy to Live in an Age of Plenty"
"In the Glorious Absence of Gods"
"Lost Things"
"Ode to *Amoeba proteus*"

"The Painted Beasts of Lascaux"
"The Reinvention of the Human Hand"
"Three Anthropomorphic Studies"
"Twenty-One Days with a Baboon Heart"

IT DOESN'T HAVE A NAME, BUT...
IT MAKES A GREAT PET!
*AND WHEN IT TOUCHES YOU, YOU CAN SEE THE ENTIRE COSMOS!

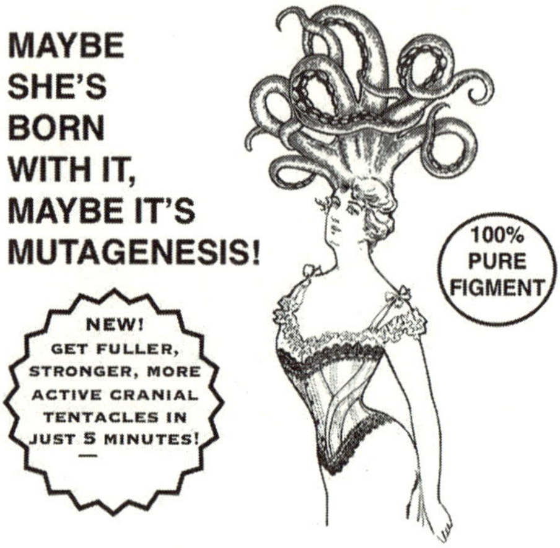
MAYBE SHE'S BORN WITH IT, MAYBE IT'S MUTAGENESIS!
NEW! GET FULLER, STRONGER, MORE ACTIVE CRANIAL TENTACLES IN JUST 5 MINUTES!
100% PURE FIGMENT

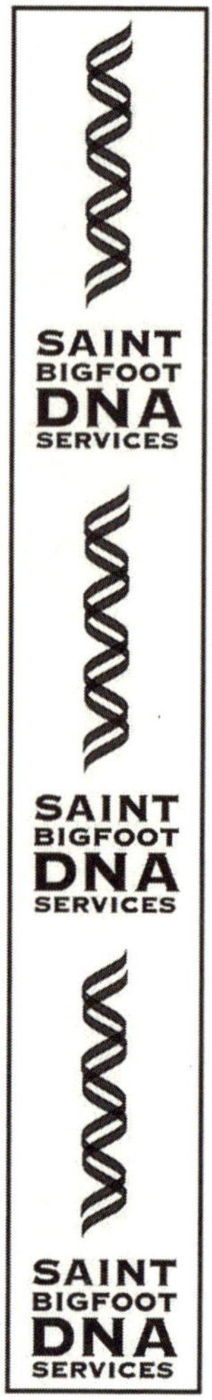
SAINT BIGFOOT DNA SERVICES
SAINT BIGFOOT DNA SERVICES
SAINT BIGFOOT DNA SERVICES

PAID ADVERTISEMENTS

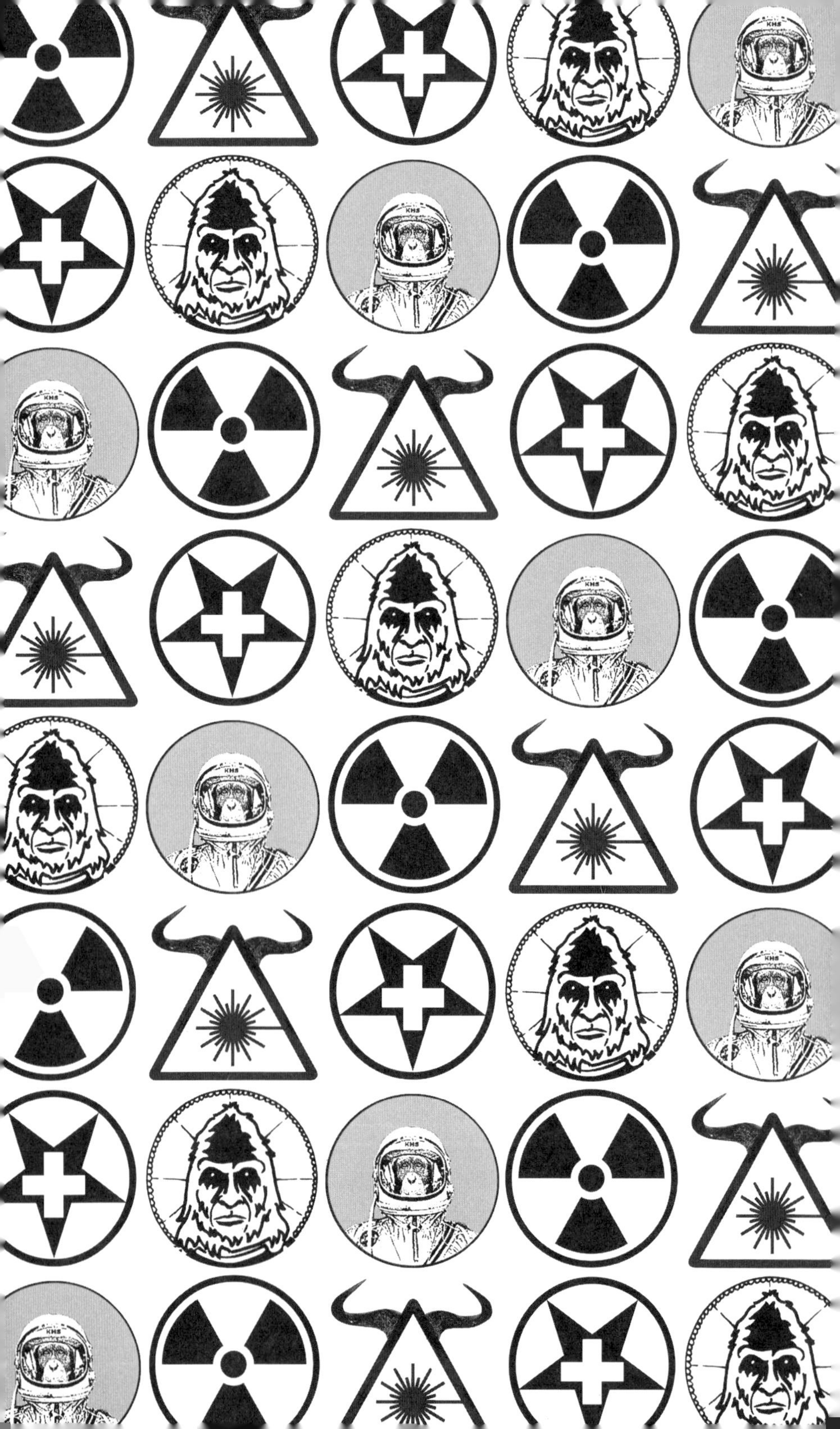